Style, Meaning and Pedagogy

Rachid Acim
Ibn Zohr University, Agadir, Morocco

Series in Education

Copyright © 2025 Vernon Press, an imprint of Vernon Art and Science Inc, on behalf of the author.

All rights reserved. No part of this publication may be reproduced, stored in a retrieval system, or transmitted in any form or by any means, electronic, mechanical, photocopying, recording, or otherwise, without the prior permission of Vernon Art and Science Inc.

www.vernonpress.com

In the Americas:
Vernon Press
1000 N West Street, Suite 1200
Wilmington, Delaware, 19801
United States

In the rest of the world:
Vernon Press
C/Sancti Espiritu 17,
Malaga, 29006
Spain

Series in Education

Library of Congress Control Number: 2024946671

ISBN: 979-8-8819-0112-7

Also available: 979-8-8819-0040-3 [Hardback]; 979-8-8819-0111-0 [PDF, E-Book]

Product and company names mentioned in this work are the trademarks of their respective owners. While every care has been taken in preparing this work, neither the authors nor Vernon Art and Science Inc. may be held responsible for any loss or damage caused or alleged to be caused directly or indirectly by the information contained in it.

Cover design by Vernon Press. Image by JL G from Pixabay.

Every effort has been made to trace all copyright holders, but if any have been inadvertently overlooked the publisher will be pleased to include any necessary credits in any subsequent reprint or edition.

To my beloved mother

with Love.

Table of Contents

	List of Tables	vii
	List of Figures	vii
	Acknowledgements	ix
	Abbreviations	xi
	General Introduction	xii
	Part I: LITERARY TEXTS	1
Chapter 1	STYLE AND THE POETIC EXPRESSION	3
Chapter 2	SEMANTIC AND PRAGMATIC MEANINGS IN "ABOU BEN ADHEM"	11
Chapter 3	CONCEPTUAL METAPHORS AND RHETORIC: "HOW DO I LOVE THEE?"	19
Chapter 4	A TRANSITIVITY PROCESS ANALYSIS OF "MANNERS"	27
Chapter 5	AN ABERRANT DECODING OF "MEMORY"	35
Chapter 6	AFRO-AMERICAN "DREAMS": A CONSTRUCTIVIST APPROACH	43
Chapter 7	READER-RESPONSE THEORY: EXPLORING STUDENTS' SENSE OF CREATIVITY	51
Chapter 8	THE PANDEMIC HOME IN PANDEMIC POETRY: "AND THE PEOPLE STAYED HOME"	69
Chapter 9	LECTURING AND LEARNING STYLES: A MEDIEVAL CLASSROOM	83

	Part II: NON-LITERARY TEXTS	99
Chapter 10	**STUDENTS' VOICES ABOUT "HEADLINES AND BLURBS"**	101
Chapter 11	**RHETORICAL TROPES: "THE NEW YORK TIMES"**	113
	General Conclusion	129
	List of References	133
	Answer Key	147
	Glossary	155
	Index	163

List of Tables

Table 4.1: Verbal Process Clauses	29
Table 4.2: Mental Process Clauses	30
Table 4.3: Material Process Clauses	31
Table 4.4: Relational Process Clauses	32
Table 7.1: Students' creative reactions to "Thinking"	58
Table 7.2: Frequency of pronouns used in the sample	64
Table 9.1: The characteristics of the social actors and event	91
Table 9.2: The metafunctions of the painting and their associated meanings	93

List of Figures

Figure 3.1: Entailment in E.B. Browning's "How Do I Love Thee?" (adapted from Lakoff & Johnson, 1980)	23
Figure 8.1: Maslow's (1943) pyramid of hierarchy needs	75
Figure 8.2: The register and contextual parameters (see Flowerdew, 2013)	77
Figure 9.1: "Liber ethicorum" des Henricus de Alemannia Staatliche Museen zu Berlin, Kupferstichkabinett / Jörg P. Anders [Public Domain Mark 1.0]	88

Acknowledgements

I would like to express my sincere thanks to the Vernon Press team, namely the commissioning editor, Blanca Caro, and the assistant editor, Irene Benavides, who kindly provided much guidance and assistance during the preparation of this book. I would like to extend my thanks to the anonymous peer reviewers for their insightful remarks, helpful suggestions and prompting feedback. I am also so much obliged to my family, my former teachers, my colleagues, students and friends. Throughout these years, and along my educational path, I have learnt a lot from the people around me. Last but not least, I am very much grateful to p.p. Ulla Prigge for helping me obtain a licence to use Voltolina's painting, "Liber ethicorum" des Henricus de Alemannia, Staatliche Museen zu Berlin, Kupferstichkabinett / Jörg P. Anders [Public Domain Mark 1.0]. To all these people in Morocco and abroad, I reiterate my deepest gratitude and appreciation.

Abbreviations

EFL	English as a Foreign Language
ELT	English Language Teaching
IFG	Introduction to Functional Grammar
MDA	Multimodal Discourse Approach
NYT	New York Times
Op-Eds	Opposite Editorials
SF	Systemic Functional
SFG	Systemic Functional Grammar
SFL	Systemic Functional Linguistics

General Introduction

Among the definitions given to Stylistics is that it is concerned with the study and examination of style in human language. This definition, however, remains problematic because style per se yields different meanings to different people at different times and places. Style can be anything that human beings do or say in order to gain appreciation and recognition from their counterparts in the vast world.

Style can be the clothes one is wearing right now; the way a person would comb his/her hair to get prepared for a wedding party; rituals at a funeral or in a graduation ceremony; how orators and TV speakers present themselves in front of their large or small public. It designates the table manners we have, knowingly or unknowingly, developed in our homes while eating with our families and friends; the smart expressions and benign emotions fluctuating in a poem; a well-crafted academic essay; the vibrant colours of a spectacular painting; a crystal trimmed chandelier; the typeface of a headline in a newspaper or the blurb shimmering on the jacket of a book.

Very simply and more uprightly, style is a gem; it encapsulates a number of skills such as reading and writing as well as thinking. In the words of the American literary scholar Michael Meyer:

> Style is everywhere around us. The world is saturated with styles in cars, clothing, buildings, teaching, dancing, music, politics – in anything that reflects a distinctive manner of expression or design. Consider, for example, how a tune sung by the Beatles differs from the same tune performed by a string orchestra. There's no mistaking the two styles. (Meyer, 1996, p. 244)

There is all the time a certain purpose, declared or undeclared, that forces people to choose one style of behaviour and bypass another. As a student, think of the manner in which you had presented your exam sheet in the exam hall at school or at your university institution. For sure, you wanted to outshine your peers and rank the top of the list in your class. You wanted to earn good grades; hence, you might be worried about which words to include and which to exclude. I bet you had scaffolded your thoughts and squeezed them into elegant ideas. In certain situations, you might be resorting to the corrector pen and colours. In others, you might embellish the content of your paper with powerful imagery and tropes so as to receive a positive feedback from your tutors and examiners. This feedback is what style is all about.

Writers and speakers cannot do without feedback. They are always inclined to choose and select from the language repertoire to impress upon others. When there is no feedback, there is certainly something wrong with style. This is the reason why some people would break up with conventions and periodically deviate from the norm. The bad news is that people would decline some styles that do not appeal to them. But the good news is that style is acquired and accessible to everyone. It does not demand a special genius; it demands diligence and regular practice. As the old adage goes: "Practice makes perfect."

The book in your hands, *Style, Meaning and Pedagogy: A Handbook for Students*, seeks to achieve two major goals: to help you grasp the intricate and slippery notion of style in English language and to show you how to critically read and approach English texts -- literary and non-literary. This dialectic relationship between style and meaning within the classroom sphere is the principal subject of this book. While it brings, on the one hand, Literary Criticism and Stylistics closer to each other, this book advocates for a strong collaboration between Discourse Studies and Pedagogy, on the other, striving hard to fill any methodological lacuna left in the literature. (van Dijk, 1981; Janks & Locke, 2008; Warriner & Anderson, 2017; Bonyadi, 2019) It emanated from the classroom debates and rich discussions I had with my undergraduate students in the Stylistics course and postgraduate students of the Applied Linguistics & ELT Master Program at Ibn Zohr University. These students frequently encounter a plethora of challenges whenever they search for meanings. They are sometimes daunted by the kind of theoretical approach or methodological procedure they have to follow in order to understand and analyze texts effectively.

The book, which shares a similar vision with other books such as Dominic Rainsford's *Studying English Literature* (Routledge, 2014) and Robert Eaglestone's *Doing English* (4th Edition, Routledge, 2018), and fits quite well in courses such as Humane Education, Creative Writing, Genre Analysis, Rhetorical Studies, to mention but a handful, can be advantageous to students pursuing their English Studies in Higher Education of either stream: Literature and Applied Linguistics. It juggles literary and non-literary texts, critical stylistics and discourse analysis, the teacher and students' reflections, to encourage the search for meaning, which obviously plays a central role in human life and human communication as a whole. Since Plato, philosophers of language have viewed this quest as the activity which brings value to our existence. (Karlsson et al., 2004)

Whether you are an undergraduate student or a classroom practitioner, and whether you are passionate about poetry criticism or media discourse, the carefully selected chapters can take you on a voyage to explore writers'

General Introduction xv

standpoints on a wide range of topics such as love, manners, home, dreams and other subsidiary themes like motivation, memory and migration. Thanks to their social relevance and significance, these particular themes are useful to university students' lives as long as they can enrich their academic and personal experiences. They are intended to prompt exploration of some human values, authors and their characters as well as opinions and reactions to them. Indubitably, the exploration of such themes will pave the ground for students to develop analogical reasoning and allow them, as Granath (2009) posits, to encounter real language rather than 'made-up examples.'

In Part I, the focus exposes the reader to literary texts, namely the enchanting power of poetry -- from Leigh Hunt to Langston Hughes, moving through Elisabeth Barrett Browning and Yeats to contemporary poets such as Kitty O'Meara, and from creative writing to painting. Again, the objective is to make the students conscious of the evolving nature of poetry across different eras and historical contexts so as to be more informed of its themes, genres and trends. Some popular texts have been proposed to enable them to comprehend the poetic style and unleash their academic imagination when dealing with its nuts and bolts.

With respect to Chapter One, the concept of style and the poetic expression are disambiguated to allow for the explication of the subsequent poems of the book. Definitions of poetry and its major trends, notably Romanticism and Neo-classicism, have been included with the view to rendering this genre quite lucid and intelligible to the prospective reader. Because meaning is fundamental to poetry writing, and since it is all the time eclipsed in its verse and rhythmical text, it is more adequate that I address the semantic and pragmatic features of "About Ben Adhem" in Chapter Two. The choice of this poem is ascribed to the fact that it endorses the idea of love and dwells on a narrative tone that sparks interest and appeals to the human ear.

Chapter Three is not different from its antecedent as it uncovers conceptual metaphors and rhetoric in "How Do I Love Thee? Let me Count the Ways." The chapter in question revolves around the types of metaphors that are closely bound up with ardent love; it discusses indexicality and again touches upon the mystery of meaning from a female perspective. Moreover, communicativeness and the sense of friendliness between human beings and other species are expounded in Chapter Four. Here, my focus is fully centred on the analysis of transitivity and process clauses of "Manners." Both the cooperative principle and the confusion surrounding the dichotomy of objectivity and subjectivity are developed as they relate to the problematic of meaning.

Chapter Five attempts to decipher "Memory" using aberrant reading, a concept which was very popular in fields such as semiotics, communication studies and journalism. Besides offering reflections on the notion of beauty and face, the chapter advances some insights about denotation and connotation as two principal methods which can be deployed to describe the meaning of words. Following the same line of thought, Chapter Six appropriates the constructivist approach in the exploration of "Dreams" and aspirations of Afro-American writers such as Langston Hughes and Martin Luther King, Jr. In my examination of this theme, I account for the phenomenon of dialogism and intertextuality, which have been integrated to transmit writers' yearnings for and desires for a brighter future.

Chapter Seven grapples with reader-response theory and students' creativity that is triggered by motivational poetry. Unlike other chapters, this one, availing itself of a bottom-up approach, reflects upon students' responsive readings of "Thinking" and investigates the metaphors they have carefully selected to promote positivity and optimism in their lives. In Chapter Eight, I explore the same issues in another genre of poetry that flourished during the global lockdown and the COVID-19 pandemic. My analytical reading of the lockdown poem, "And the People Stayed Home", aimed at providing another definition of home and explaining how the private space satisfied people's lower and higher needs. Along with register and contextual factors, a mixed stylistic approach has been employed to dismantle the home of the pandemic and elucidate the ancient relationship between poetry and healing.

Chapter Nine deals with lecture-based instruction and learning styles in a medieval painting. The significance of the chapter resides in the fact that it introduces the reader to other facets of style, whose contours appear in the two processes of teaching and learning. My objective is to show the pedagogical functions of art and to equip the readers with a toolkit so that they can understand and analyze visual texts in a systematic way.

Part II is devoted exclusively to non-literary texts such as headlines, blurbs and news stories since these texts have been neglected and marginalized in the EFL and Stylistics classroom, which developed a long predilection and proclivity towards literature. In Chapter Ten, I bring to the fore students' voices about the language of "headlines" and "blurbs." Whereas the headlines address the topic of human migration and refugees, the blurb discusses the pleasures of poetry. After describing the stylistic features of either discourse, some practical tips and signposts have been suggested to assist readers in their critical analyses of texts having a commercial tinge.

Chapter Eleven is approximately an extension of the previous chapter because it engages a rhetorical analysis of the persuasive devices and stylistic tropes that are privileged by the writers of the New York Times in their representation of certain minorities and social groups. On returning to the functions of language, I emphasize that the journalistic discourse, whether it appertains to tabloids or broadsheets, cannot do without selections. This chapter is of paramount importance, for it tends to raise the readers' awareness about the rhetorical dimensions of language, its eloquent features, and the possible ways they can draw upon to detect bias and subjectivity in human discourse.

What is at stake is that such amalgamation of texts and a variety of chapters are more likely to enhance the readers' comprehension and analytical skills and convince them to draw analogies concerning creativity in terms of language use or style in general. This variety, I argue, will help the students learn to apply multiple approaches and methods when analyzing or interpreting increasingly difficult texts, written or visual. Observes Nunan (2017, p. 148), "Variety is the spice of life, and a variety of different text types will serve to maintain interest and motivation." The Highlights' sections, alongside Further Readings and the Questions suggested for discussion, endeavour to enlarge their scope of thinking about the topics of the texts and to get them to compensate for any flaws or weaknesses as far as comprehension or explication are concerned.

In connection with the genres of the texts, the following points should be noted: the majority of works explicated relate to narrative and lyric as well as pandemic and motivational poetry, each of which varies in length and difficulty; a few, for the sake of variety, though standing seemingly short and concise, they doubtlessly stimulate one's mind.

Rachid Acim is an Associate Professor of English and Discourse Analysis at the Faculty of Letters & Human Sciences (FLHS), Ibn Zohr University, Agadir, Morocco.

Part I:
LITERARY TEXTS

Chapter 1

STYLE AND THE POETIC EXPRESSION

> **Highlights:**
> - *Style is problematic, slippery and very elusive.*
> - *It involves selection in terms of vocabulary and tropes.*
> - *It is abstract and concrete, and it is present everywhere.*
> - *There are three views of style: the monist, the dualist and the pluralist.*
> - *Style can be dismantled by looking at six rubrics.*

1.1 Introduction

This chapter revolves around the hardships scholars encounter when they resolve to define or identify style. The diversity of disciplines where style lingers on implies that style is slippery and quite problematic, for there is a lack of compromise concerning its definition and common features. By tracking down the historical roots of style, researchers, whether they are students or professors, can stay more focused on its purpose and functions. Aside from the problem of definitions structured here below, debates are still going on in academia with respect to the major components of style, the efficient theories and methodologies that can systematically account for style, and why style is all the time overlapping with the poetic expression. My aim here is to propose a toolkit for all stakeholders so as to experiment with style and learn about its evolution and ancient linkage to poetry.

1.2 Operational Definitions

Etymologically, the concept style was conceived of as a tool that was utilized in writing, hence the term (*stylus*), i.e., a kind of pen, and later it designated the 'fashion of writing.' Let us sketch out some heterogeneous definitions that are frequently employed by stylisticians and experts of language to define style:

- "At its simplest, style refers to the perceived distinctive manner of expression in writing or speaking, just as there is a perceived manner of doing things, like playing squash or painting. We might talk of someone writing in an 'ornate style', or speaking in a 'comic style.' For some people, as for Aristotle, style has evaluative connotations: style can be good or bad." (Wales, 2011, p. 397)

- "By style is meant the constant form – and sometimes the constant elements, qualities, and expression – in the art of an individual or a group." (Schapiro, 1961, p. 51)
- "Style refers to the manner of doing things." (Baker & Ellece, 2011, p. 141)
- "A concept that has been used in cultural and media studies mainly with respect to youth subcultures to characterize dress, language, taste, and so on." (Abercrombie & Longhurst, 2007, p. 330)

The common denominator between these aforementioned definitions is that they showcase that style serves as a medium through which people establish connections with the external world.

More frequently, style is used in reference to fashionable elegance, smartness, distinctiveness and eminence. From a linguistic perspective, scholars have specified three views of style: the dualist view, the monist view and the pluralist view. (Short, 1996; Leech & Short, 2007) Regarding the dualist view, form and meaning were seen as separate and style was defined as a dress of thought. In what concerns the monist view, style (form) and meaning were seen both as interlinked and inseparable, and that a choice of form presupposes a selection of meaning. As for the pluralist view, it claimed that 'language performs a number of different functions, and any piece of language is likely to be the result of choices made on different functional levels." (Leech & Short, 2007, p. 24)

For Cuddon (1998), style alludes to the characteristic manner of expression in prose or verse; how a certain author expresses his/her views about things. The analysis and assessment of style entails the examination of a writer's choice of words, his/her figures of speech, the tropes (rhetorical and otherwise), the shape/size of the paragraphs – every aspect of language and the way it was presented. Though it is somewhat easy to describe style, assessing it remains a daunting job because it is the tone and 'voice' of the author; as peculiar to him as his/her laugh, his/her walk, his/her handwriting and the expressions on his/her face. Sometimes, styles are roughly classified into several categories: (a) according to period: Metaphysical, Augustan, Georgian, etc.; (b) according to individual authors: Chaucerian, Miltonic, Gibbonian, Jamesian, etc.; (c) according to level: grand, middle, low and plain; and (d) according to language: scientific, expository, poetic, emotive, referential, journalistic, etc.

Owing to the obscurity of the stylistic approach and the methodology that researchers are required both to follow and apply when approaching style, and because practitioners of Stylistics themselves agree that the concept itself is nebulous and fuzzy, six broad rubrics have been suggested to help students and researchers draft their stylistic analyses: (1) style as deviation from a norm; (2) a manifestation of the individual; (3) content and/or form; (4) choice between alternative ways of expressing the same idea; (5) product of context; and (6) good or beautiful writing. (Azuike, 1992) All these rubrics will be detailed and explored further in the next chapters of this book. First, let us provide a sketchy view about the most popular trends in poetry.

1.3 Popular Trends in Poetry

One of the areas where style was used creatively and artistically is poetry composition. Sound, imagery and word play are key stylistic mechanisms and vehicles for poets. Authors of poetry construct meaning through the careful selection of poetic devices, such as metaphor and alliteration, to create vivid imagery and rhyme for a resonating sound. (Johnson 2024) Almost in each culture and civilization, poets have produced incredible styles to express their individual and collective emotions vis-a-vis the status quo. In the period ranging from 1800 to 1850, Romantic poets, for instance, have allowed people to travel beyond themselves to discover unusual experiences of grandeur and sublimity. The period coincided with the time at which Britain industrialized itself. Many factories were set up in towns and cities across the country, and the agricultural mode of living people had known for centuries stopped being taken at face value.

Although the concept is today restricted to valentine's day, candlelit nights and the exchange of boxes of chocolates, some writers belonging to this trend were dismissed by their opposition to the rationalism of the Enlightenment, some by the ideals of the French Revolution, others by their attraction to and fascination with "sublime" natural phenomena – mountains, rivers, storms – and still others by the various wonders of Orientalism and the East. (Maunder, 2010) Many times, Romanticism, as a literary school and movement, was revised, forsaken, resurrected and parodied by journalists and academics on account of the variety of meanings it yields to people. It is possible that this is one reason why an ancient scholar aired these words to clarify the concept:

> Romanticism is the weeping star; it is the sighing wind, the chilly night, the bird in its flight, and the sweet-scented flower; it is the refreshing stream, the greatest ecstasy, the well by the palm trees, rosy hope and her thousand lovers, the angel and the pearl, the robe of the willows. (Ferber, 2010, p. 3)

Unlike Neoclassicals who glorified intellect and reason, the Romantics praised emotions and sensations since they were the products of the heart. As Høystad (2007, p. 191) observes, "In Romanticism, the heart becomes a symbol of most of what the age stands for. The period has got its name directly from the literary genre, the *romance* that the age of chivalry cultivated."

Imagination was an essential feature of the Romantic Movement and it marked the poetry of Romantic poets such as John Keats (1795-1821), Samuel Taylor Coleridge (1772-1834), Percy Bysshe Shelley (1792-1822) and others. As a spiritual force, imagination was closely bound up with ethics and morality. When deployed to the world of literature, and to poetry in particular, imagination provided ample alternatives for the improvement of the human life and its humdrumness. For Romantic poets, imagination was considered as a peculiar faculty of the heart as it permits a better comprehension of that truth which transcends the human mind and intellect:

> The poet leads the reader into a world which in character is profound, religious, ultimate, and which, but for the poet's imagination, must have remained inaccessible. According to this view, the imagination yields insight into a world that is transcendental or supersensible in its nature. The implication is that there are two worlds, the one available to ordinary people in possession of the usual senses, and the other open only to those who have the imagination or genius to see it. (Diffey, 2016, p. 172)

The style crafted by the Romantics was characterized by the love of Mother Nature because Mother Nature was viewed as a haven and a source of inspiration for them. It brought symmetry to the poet's character, psyche and soul; it restored order and stability to his/her broken heart, which reportedly suffered loneliness, grief, separation, sorrow and melancholy. Each element of Mother Nature had much significance for the Romantic poet as long as it imparts jubilation, serenity and peace of mind. "Live in the sunshine, swim the sea, drink the wild air," reminds us of the founding father of Transcendentalism, Ralph Waldo Emerson (1803- 1882), who was both influenced and inspired by the European Romantic Movement of the eighteenth and nineteenth centuries.

The most acceptable poetic themes making up the core of the Romantic style were not only human but also divine. The traditional topics were the sun and the moon, angels, stars, maids, a lake, the earth, the Heavens, a nightingale, a cliff, tombs, a rose, nymphs, mountain, a castle, a mistress, hares, and the lake. All these elements were well-known and commonly used by the Romantic poets. Even their dreams and hopes were prohibited from diverging from the conventional path. The Romantics, as Maunder (2010) notes, also had a special interest in culture, myths, the arts, and mysteries of the ancient world, inspired partly by the French general Napoleon Bonaparte's failed bid to conquer Egypt and partly by a revived interest in the classics of ancient Greece and Rome.

Modern poetry, nonetheless, creates a short story, with visual imagery, in a few lines rather than lengthy poems. Ezra pound's (1885-1972) "In a Station of the Metro" provides such concrete example of a new genre of poetry that models itself after the Japanese haiku since it was succinct and condensed. In this particular poem, Pound catches a moment in the underground metro station in the French capital in 1910. Being so intrigued by this uncommon visual scene, he decided to subsume the faces of the individuals in the metro in his poem, drawing on a meticulous description and a complex equation.

Not different from Romantic poetry though, the most common themes for the modern one are love and romance, nature, beauty, loss and grief. These are the things that everyone can relate to and identify with, and when written in the versified form, with modern language use, a poem can bring about feelings long forgotten, remind of times of strong emotion, or speak of dreams for the future. (Constantine, 2012) According to Lawrenson et al. (1969, p. 149): "Modern poetry draws at once from painting, music, statuary, arabesque art, philosophic raillery, and the analytic spirit; and so happily, so skillfully adjusted that it presents itself with visible signs of a subtlety borrowed from diverse arts."

Remarkably, poets have excelled in the construction of imaginary worlds to transport their readers from monotony into excitement and rebirth. The 'elsewhere' of the poem, to quote Robinson (2002, p. 70), "can only exist if it simultaneously maps, point for point, onto 'here.'" This imaginative space and time of the poem can be exploited to fully grasp the poet's past experiences and thus benefit the present life of his/her readers. Put differently, the poem approaches the life of the past and brings it vividly to a contemporary audience offering them the adequate expertise to critically examine their lives and study the social values that govern their day-to-day experiences. Poetry is thus a unique resource for people who are much concerned with teaching and learning, dialogue and reconciliation, therapy and healing, compassion and empathy, diversity and even the question of difference. A question that poses itself here remains: "What is poetry?" A difficult question, as we shall see in the coming chapters.

1.4 What is Poetry?

Many years ago, Samuel Taylor Coleridge (1772-1834) suggested that poetry is the most scrumptious words presented in the best order. His fellow, William Wordsworth (1770-1850), considered it the unprompted abundance of powerful emotions. Whereas, T.S. Eliot (1888- 1965) famously declared that "poetry is not a turning loose of emotion, but an escape from emotion; it is not the expression of personality, but an escape from personality." (Eliot, 2010, p. 92) In turn, Leigh Hunt (1784-1859) defined poetry quite comprehensively as "a passion for power, because power is impression triumphant, whether over the poet, as desired by himself, or over the reader, as affected by the poet." (Jesson-Dibley, 2003, p. 64) In fact, poetry is a yearning to explore truth and beauty, which are represented sophisticatedly through the medium of language and the beguiling force of imagination. Still, one might venture that poetry is hard to delimit, yet poets have consented that any definition should start, as Pomorska & Rudy (1987) note, by juxtaposing what poetry is to what it is not.

Poetry requires a different approach from the one used for ordinary or prosaic texts. The spontaneous overflow of emotions, the beauty of metaphorical symbols and images, acute expressions, and the good arrangement of lexes and dictions, are what accords poetry with this literary power and stylistic majesty. In structure and content, poetry tells us that there is always more, there is always a surplus of meaning. (McIntosh & Warren, 2013) Merton and Hark (1985) seem to agree with this:

> In poetry, words are charged with meaning in a far different way than are the words in a piece of scientific prose. The words of a poem are not merely the signs of concepts: they are also rich in affective and spiritual associations. The poet uses words not merely to make declarations, statement of fact. That usually the last thing that concerns him. He seeks above all to put words together in such a way that they exercise a mysterious and vital reactivity among themselves, and so release their secret associations to produce in the reader an experience that enriches the depths of his spirit in a manner quite unique. (p. 27)

As is the case for art, poetry addresses people's psychological needs, and it caters to their expectations and emotional wants. People enjoy art, especially if it connects with them; they are prone to chronicle their experiences through artistic expression such as painting and drawing. The same thing applies to poetry. When it matches people's experiences, it appeals to them. To get their meaning across in a more vivid and insightful way, poets very often invest in a number of rhetorical and stylistic devices like comparisons, metaphors, similes and exaggerations. (Mahony, 2003) These devices sometimes obscure the meanings of the poem and puzzle poetry readers and listeners.

1.5 Conclusion

In this chapter, I have attempted to provide some working definitions of style and elucidated that this concept remains debatable for scholars and researchers working in the field. I then cast some light on the art of poetry because it is regarded as the point of departure for stylisticians since its language keeps baffling and attracting people to it. The discussion has also covered how some poets viewed poetry and detailed on its most popular trends and schools. When readers become cognizant of the major movements that shaped poetry writing along history, they will face less trouble talking about its cryptic meanings and knotty style. The next chapter attempts to demarcate the semantic and pragmatic meanings in a narrative poem bearing the name of "Abou Ben Adhem."

1.6 Further Readings

Bradford, R. (1997). *Stylistics*. London and New York: Routledge.

Chan, C. S. (1993). Operational definitions of style, *Environment and planning B: Planning and design*, 21 (2), pp. 223-246, https://doi.org/10.1068/b210223

Crystal, D., & Davy, D. (1969). *Investigating English style*. London: Longman.

Genova, J. (1979). The significance of style. *The journal of aesthetics and art criticism*, 37 (3), pp. 315-324, https://doi.org/10.2307/430785

Giovanelli, M. (2010). Pedagogical stylistics: A text world theory approach to the teaching of poetry, *English in Education*, 44 (3), pp. 214-231, DOI: 10.1111/j.1754- 8845.2010 01074.x

1.7 Questions for Discussion

1) What is style in language?
2) In your opinion, why are stylisticians in disagreement whenever they endeavor to define the concept of style?
3) Is style abstract or concrete? Is it both? Give illustrations from real life to support your answer.
4) How did the Romantic poets view style in poetry? Why did they stress the centrality of the heart? What about the Neoclassicals? Cite two different poems where you show differences and similarities (if any) between either trend.
5) Why is aesthetics always associated with style and evoked in Stylistics?
6) Can you think of three essential ways, by dint of which poets can demonstrate their creativity in poetry writing and composition?

Chapter 2

SEMANTIC AND PRAGMATIC MEANINGS IN "ABOU BEN ADHEM"

Highlights:

- *The poem is an endorsement of the spirit of fellowship.*
- *Two patterns of love permeate in the poem: horizontal (human) and vertical (divine).*
- *The poem appertains to the narrative genre.*
- *There is an abundance of static and dynamic verbs.*
- *Features such as repetition, alliteration and parallelism have been foregrounded by the poet.*

2.1 Introduction

This chapter offers university students of humane education and beyond some insights into narrative poetry. It addresses the representation of love as perceived by the British poet and essayist Leigh Hunt (1784-1859) in his luminous poem "Abou Ben Adhem." The chapter is inspired by the Russian formalist theory of foregrounding, which comes to mean 'defamiliarization' (ostranenie, i.e., 'estrangement' or 'making strange'), a theory that was inaugurated into literary criticism by Victor Shklovsky (1893-1984). Two aims are considered here: (a) I unpack the language features of the poem at the semantic and pragmatic levels, and I untangle the conundrum of love and showcase why it is essential to human dialogue and peace.

2.2 Endorsing the Spirit of Fellowship

The subject matter of Leigh Hunt's poem "Abou Ben Adhem" is a commitment to humanity, yet the most dominant theme has to do with love, peace and fellowship as expressed by the Sufi practitioner. From the very outset, the speaker seems attracted to and fascinated by Abou's personality, whose name has reoccurred in the poem (n=5). This strong fascination and mesmerism by Abou's character is tacitly clear in the heartfelt invocation voiced by the speaker to proliferate and reduplicate the likes of this noble man in the world. Note when he said in line 1: (may his tribe increase!).

This plea is evocative of the speaker's aspiration for love and peace to be prevalent over hate and conflicts. What he is eclipsing is that the world appears governed by egomania and self-centeredness, which supposedly bring about division and disharmony between people. That he has referred to "peace" in line 2 is not at all fortuitous because it might serve as a leitmotif that a certain tragedy is taking place somewhere. The corollary of this is that the speaker sustains a daydream about love, friendship and peace. Peace refers not only to pacification and conciliation, but also encompasses the psychological troubles and imbalance undergone by certain people inside and not outside.

It is true that the speaker keeps searching for peace outside the precincts of the poem, but the fact that he brought "Abou" to speak from his dream of it pinpoints that he is primarily concerned with looking for esoteric peace inside humanity itself. By describing the dream in-depth, he vehicles the idea that this is not an ordinary dream -- a dream that lapses just for a short span of time; rather, the dream in question, is super-ordinary and unusual because it is accessible only to God's saints and chosen people.

2.3 The Process of Narrativity

The narrative style proffers the poem a spiritual and emotional force. The inclusion of the past simple tense gives the impression that the poet is recounting a human story that seemingly a certain individual has experienced in his life time. It is called for to describe its characters and, at the same time, classify its sequential events and render them more tangible to potential readers. As a matter of fact, it is predominantly used "to describe past happenings" (Burke, 2014, p. 203), which might be real or unreal. Again, what is important here is how tense, or "past historic", to use Gönczöl-Davies' (2008) words, is constantly and consistently exploited to represent this unique multiple perspective on events and to invite the reader into sharing it.

Constative verbs like "awoke" and "saw" or performative ones such as "raised" and "answered" are suggestive of an interaction or a speech act that is taking place inside and outside the poem. The verb "saw", for example, is very powerful in that it channels the reader to think that reality itself is embedded in the dream, that the speaker, and so is Abou, is neither weaving nor making up this story from their proper imagination or subjective reflection. Moreover, the insertion of the imperative form at the end (line 14), when Abou kindly requested the angel to write his name in the list of God's lovers, presumably, breaks the tone of the narratorial discourse of the poem. This shift into the utilization of the imperative is probably more common in verse than in prose;

however, the effects are similar. (Black, 2006) As is the case with direct speech acts, the reader is drawn into the discourse situation of the poem, and this creates emphatic involvement.

Although the dream is narrated in an uncomplicated fashion, the poet enriches it by developing other subsidiary themes that somehow contribute to the poem's beautiful architecture and stylistic design. Effective human communication is easily spotted throughout, yet altruism, good faith and devotion to God cannot be overlooked in almost every line. These themes as far as the poet is concerned, are as important as love and devotion to humanity. This is explored through the employment of metaphorical expressions, tropes and figurative language, which both the setting and the interactants necessitate. With respect to the social setting, the reader is informed that it is a room; however, it is not rendered in bombastic terms or described in an extravagant manner.

It is obvious that the poet is not interested in a physical portraying of the place because he is more focused on the mystical character involved in it. To approximate the place to the reader's mind and imagination, the poet has deployed a simile; hopefully, this stylistic and rhetorical device could help in building a mental picture of what that place looks like. In fact, it is identical to a rose in bloom, and it is luminous on the grounds of the ethereal light that was showered in the room. Such ethereal light not only does it implant life into the room, but also makes it spiritually richer and more worthwhile than other earthly rooms. If the second is man-made, the first is unmistakably heavenly and divine.

In line 5, the poet introduces another character that was also present in the room, silently engaged in accomplishing a serious divine mission. Unlike Abou, this character is not identified by name, nor is it defined by any specific quality, gender or attribute. All that the reader knows about this character is that it is "an angel," who customarily writes down the names of God's lovers in a book of gold. The indefinite article "an" is indeed misleading because, on the one hand, it reveals that the poet tends to rouse the reader's interest to explore the exotic realm of the dream, and it implies that angels are prone to be a source of inspiration for Abou, on the other. They are like messengers sent by God to provide guidance and edification to His chosen people.

In line 7, the poet, assuming that the reader has already known what he was talking about and that the referent (angel) is well defined, juxtaposed the definite article "the" to the subsequent referents "Presence" (line 7), "vision" (line 8) and "angel" (line 12). Consider how Hunt's poem exploits this dichotomy of new and given information in a very creative way to involve the readers and spark their interests in the story:

> Given information refers to information which the speaker assumes to be already known to the addressee, because the latter is supposed to have found it in the linguistic or situational context of the discourse, or in the wider context of commonly shared knowledge about the world. So given information provides a kind of background to other elements of the discourse communicating new information of which the speaker assumes that the addressee cannot have acquired knowledge from one of the three contextual factors (place, time, person) mentioned above. (Verdonk, 2002, p. 37)

Given the speaker's burgeoning interest in the conversation between Abou and the angel, he resolved to front some metaphorical images to ease the understanding of the dream. One metaphorical image that starkly emerges therein is that of an angel who was writing in a book of gold. The special reference to gold is thought to function much like a reference to supernatural entities that are not within the reach of people. This fascination with gold is as old as civilization itself.

> The ancient Egyptians esteemed gold, which had religious significance to them, and King Tuthankhamun was buried in a solid-gold coffin 3300 years ago. The wandering Israelites worshipped a golden calf, and the legendary King Midas asked that everything he touched be turned into gold. (Wallace & Prabhu, 1975, p. 25)

It is crystal clear that the poet chose the metaphor of gold because gold is extremely beautiful, easy to work with, and it is, like style, particularly important for ornamentation and embellishment. That the angel writes in a book of gold connotes that what he is writing is highly significant, as nobody is permitted to detect what he is writing, and that, after all, such writing will not rust or corrode despite the passing of time. More or less like gold and style, this writing is stupendous, durable and indestructible.

2.4 Parts of Speech

The paraverbal elements, along with the prosodic features that accompanied the exchanges (the vision raised / Abou spoke / But cheerily still / and said) imply that the poet is paying succinct attention to minor details to develop them into a complete vision, which both denaturalizes and defamiliarizes the dream. In his estrangement of the dream, the poet had resorted to intertextuality and allusion when registering and narrating it down through his verse. Direct quoting, as one form of intertextuality, actualizes the dream as well as invigorates it; so the dream does not appear distant or remote, but rather it becomes more proximate either in time and space. Such proximity of the dream from the reader's mental conception might drive them to be inquisitive not only about the dream but also about Abou and his ascetic life and spiritual wanderings. In so far as Matoesian (2001) is concerned,

> Direct quotes or direct speech are a central intertextual device for connecting the narrated (historical) and narrating (current) speech events. Direct quotes are a type of reported speech that minimizes the intertextual gap in the decontextualization and recontextualization of a prior spate of talk. More prosaically, direct quotes appear as an exact replica of the words spoken in historical context. They make the performed words appear close to the historical words and, in so doing, enliven those historical words, giving them an aura of objectivity and authority. (p. 110)

In addition to the presence of direct speech, which grants the poem the effect of giving the reader some time to create and build up a visual representation of the night's mysterious dream, the poem is structured as a sequence of events, where word stress falls mainly on verbs. The following chunks are illustrative of this semantic feature:

a) Awoke one night.
b) And saw, with the moonlight.
c) And to the presence...he said.
d) And with a look made.
e) And showed the names...had blest.
f) And lo! ...led all the rest.

When surveying these chunks, one will notice that the coordinating conjunction "and" was repeated at least 5 times (n=8 in the poem), which means that the poet has divided the poem into several factions, each of which collocates well with one another. The poetic balance achieved throughout, together with the pleasurable rhyme and rhythm, offers the poem much charm since it appeals to the inner ears of the reader. The way grammatical structures are arranged and words' stresses are patterned add up to the aesthetics of the poem, for it is not meant to be read silently but rather aloud. While many lexical items alliterate both vertically and horizontally like: Abou Ben Adhem / deep dream of peace / The names of those / like a lily in bloom / I pray thee, then, the rhyming pattern of couplets (AA-BB-CC-DD-EE- FF-GG-HH-II) stand out, cheering up the reader along the reading process. It may be fair to say that "[a]lliteration has a cohesive effect, since identical sounds tend to tie words together" (Nørgaard et al. 2010, p. 49), yet the rhyme scheme, as another type of sound similarity does not rhyme just to the eye but to the ear as well. (Bennett, 1999)

In order to exert a psychological effect on the reader, the poet, knowingly or unknowingly, draws on foregrounding theory, which allows him to recreate and regenerate Abou. Foregrounding, which has been defined by Simpson (2004, p. 50) as "a form of textual patterning which is motivated specifically for literary-aesthetic purposes," occurs not only in the poet's tendency to reshuffle his words but also in "making strange" some verbal structures to better sequence the events. Sometimes, this stylistic trope comes in another guise by fronting some parallel constructions like "Awoke…and saw" / "Wrote, and vanished" / "It came…and showed." At other times, it comes as repetition or "more of the same," the objective of which is producing memorable effects. Thus, the poem is easy to read and rehearse.

With respect to other parts of speech, like adjectives, they are injected into the poem since they help generate word pictures and, therefore, lead the reader to visualize the action. (Boufford, 1998) Abstract adjectives such as "rich", "deep", "bold", "sweet", and "great" are used to dress up nouns like "dream", "room", "Ben Adhem", "accord", and "wakening light." Needless to mention, except for "low" [line 12], which reiterates Abou's reverential esteem for the angel, the adjectives above add extra information to the nouns and pronouns; meanwhile, they invite the reader to connect both emotionally and spiritually with the mystery and tenor of the dream.

2.5 Pragmatic and Implied Meaning

Thematically, the love that crops up in the poem can be grouped into two major types: human / horizontal (i.e., when Abou expressed his love for his fellow men) and divine / vertical (i.e. when the angel showed the names that were blessed by God's love). These prominent categories of love predominate over the poem and provide it with a spiritual asset and mystical weight. Both patterns of love are intertwined so long as each of them is the gateway to the other. Love here is not sensual or carnal. It is highly spiritual and heavenly, instead. Not coincidental then that the speaker is borrowing many terms and expressions from the lexicon of religion with the objective of honouring Abou and adorning him with heavenly traits. The semantic field of religion is manifest in the following lexical items: "angel", "Lord", "pray", "love", "wakening", "light", and "God." In fact, all these expressions are indicative of Abou's humility, awe and devoutness. This implied meaning of terms and words requires that readers have enough knowledge of mysticism and mystical culture to understand the pragmatic meanings, all of which encapsulate human dialogue and peace. As Clark and Pointon (2016, p. 71) argue: "the implied meaning of a word is often more than its dictionary definition", which is to say that behind every single word, there lurks an allusion and a pragmatic meaning. Unlike the semantic meaning, which is a conventionalized form of meaning (Cummings, 2005), the pragmatic meaning has to put language in its social context and it hinges upon speech acts, inference and the way words are used. Dealing with speaker's/language user's meaning as well as the intent of a poem, pragmatic meaning is not an alternative but complementary to semantic meaning. (Verdonk 2002)

What is striking about Abou is that he has exerted an enormous impact on the coming Sufi mystics. Rumi (1207-1273), for example, has composed various poems about this noble figure, his renouncement of the world and ultimate leanings towards solitude and contemplation. He himself appears enchanted by Abou's life and ascetic mode of living. The former's visibility and strong presence in the poetry of Eastern and Western poets prove that he was by no means an exemplar of love, nourishing the minds and souls of so many people.

Teaching Hunt's poem "Abou Ben Adhem" is an exciting experience. Not only does it allow students to rectify their misconceptions and stereotypes about the "Other", but it also increases their curiosity to explore different cultures and look up to them. Such poetry that highlights universal values like love, peace and dialogue is strongly recommended now more than ever in classroom settings because it paves the ground for amity and mutual understanding to come to fruition. Every student should be instructed that it is only through horizontal love and togetherness that human welfare can exist.

2.6 Conclusion

In a nutshell, "Abou Ben Adhem" reflects one humanitarian sentiment that the world needs nowadays. By taking a snapshot of the dream and Abou's encounter with the angel, Hunt has conveyed that all human beings are brothers and sisters under the umbrella of humanity. He led the readers to look at love from multiple angles so that they can put it into practice when interacting with their peers. The presence of metaphorical language, the storytelling technique and the good positioning of parallel and syntactic structures, as well as the rhyming of words and sounds made the poem sophisticated and quite elegant; because of this, the reader is left to meditate over its overall moral resonating across its versified and rhythmical lines: "To earn God's love, love the board." In the chapter that follows, I lay bare the major conceptual metaphors prevalent in Elisabeth Barrett Browning's romantic poem, "How Do I Love Thee? Let Me Count the Ways."

2.7 Further Readings

Acim, R. (2021). Why narrative poetry still matters in stylistics. *Journal of educational research and practice,* 11, pp. 439 – 453, https://doi.org/10.5590/JERAP.2021.11.1.31

Field, C. (1910). Ibrahim Ben Adham. *Mystics and saints of Islam.* London: Francis Griffiths, pp. 36-45.

Jones, R. (2009). Leigh Hunt's oriental motifs: Abou Ben Adhem. *Journal of the royal Asiatic society,* 7 (3), pp. 389-397, DOI: https://doi.org/10.1017/S1356186300009421

Roe, N. (2003). *Leigh Hunt: Life, poetics, politics.* London: Routledge.

Wexler, M. (2014). A poetry program for the very elderly – Narrative perspective on one therapeutic model. *Journal of poetry therapy,* 27 (1), pp. 35-46, DOI: 10.1080/08893675.2014.871811

2.8 Questions for Discussion

1) What are the central themes that crop up in Leigh Hunt's poem "Abou Ben Adhem"?
2) In your opinion, why did the poet choose this mystical character?
3) How can you describe the style of the poem?
4) Which stylistic elements stand out in the text?
5) Can you give some examples of rhetorical devices that embellish the poem?
6) Do you think that the poem can be used in multicultural classroom settings? Explain.

Chapter 3

CONCEPTUAL METAPHORS AND RHETORIC: "HOW DO I LOVE THEE?"

Highlights:

- *Metaphors are part of human everyday life; they conceal and reveal.*
- *Indexicality refers to the idea of mentioning and pointing to.*
- *Love includes three elements: admiration, intellectual interaction and predispositions for reunion.*
- *Metaphors contribute to the achievement of closeness and intimacy.*
- *Epistemic modality expresses the mood and attitude of the speaker.*

3.1 Introduction

This chapter, which is inspired by Lakoff and Johnson's (1980) "conceptual metaphors," is relevant to students of Literary Linguistics. It probes into the dialectic relationship between metaphors and rhetoric in "How Do I Love Thee? Let Me Count The Ways" – written by the Victorian poet, Elisabeth Barrett Browning (1806-1861). In the first place, I scrutinize the phenomena of deixis and indexicality. Then, I bring to the fore the numerous metaphors that the poet appropriated to achieve intimacy and closeness with the addressee, the English poet and playwright – Robert Browning (1812-1889). Intimacy here involves proximity with people, and it designates the ability to share even the innermost emotions and private thoughts.

3.2 Metaphors We Can Think Of

Metaphors are essential for the articulation of the human feelings. They are often used to talk about things that are unprecedented and new. Sometimes, they are employed as persuasive devices, and as such, they conceal as well as reveal. (Kennedy, 2000) Aristotle described them as the medium by which the poet provides knowledge through artistic imitation (Johnson, 1981); Plato conceived them as living creatures rather than figures of speech. (Campbell, 1883) An enraged man, for example, is a lion, a cunning man is a fox, a firm man is a rock, a learned man is a torch. A lamb is innocence; a snake is a subtle spite; flowers express to us the delicate affections. Light and darkness are our familiar expression for knowledge and ignorance; and heat for love. Visible distance behind and before us, is respectively, our image of memory and hope. (qtd. In Atkinson, 1940) Before clustering the conceptual metaphors evoked by the poet, it is advantageous that we discuss the stylistic phenomena of deixis and indexicality since the speaker, and by extension the poet, is explicitly mentioning and pointing to one specific addressee.

3.3 Indexicality

The poem was composed by Elisabeth Barrett Browning around 1845-46; it featured in *Sonnets from the Portuguese* and bespoke her soulful desire to intermingle with fellow poet Robert Browning. Critics view it as one of the most often quoted poems in English. (Gadd, 2006). Its expressive power, the rhythm of its language, its resonant imagery and the elevation of its emotion project it as the greatest and the best poems ever written. Besides fostering a deep impression on the mind, it takes the readers on a memorable journey, which makes them feel they have learned something about life. (Farndon, 2014) Through the deictic pronouns "I" (n=10) and "thee" (n=9), the speaker demonstrates full engagement in a love affair, which would progress into marriage. She challenges the rigidity of the family system and the excessive authority of a father, who rules with an iron-fist denying his progeny freedom of will and choice. Poetry was the medium to reach out to the addressee, and as McLuhan (2013) states in his *Understanding Media*: the medium is the message. The transmission of E.B. Browning's love to R. Browning passes through the channel of love poetry, and there is certainly no better channel to say "I love thee" than via poetry.

Like poets of the time, E.B. Browning capitalizes on the power of rhetoric and metaphoricity to disclose her ideal love by asking and simultaneously answering the many ways she fell for her man. At first glance, this sequence, as Simpson (2004, p. 9) writes, "bears the stylistic imprint of the *lyric* poem" [italics is not mine]. This self-introspection subsumes a single voice that expresses the innermost emotions and perceptions with respect to ardent love. The addressee is not identified by any attribute, race, color, or whatsoever. His anonymity accounts for the popularity as well as the timelessness of the poem; it will last for about more than 171 years, and it will be read in wedding ceremonies and shared by lovers on different occasions. One critical reflection on the poem and its moving style reads as follows:

> In the first line the speaker expresses her desire to "count the ways" she loves. She only mentions six, a lot for a 14-line poem, sure, but not as

many as I expected. The expression of the intensity of her love, therefore, should not be measured in the quantity of expression but in the quality or depth of expression, a depth which equals "the depth and breadth and height / My soul can reach," to the level of every's / most quiet need," and a love that will continue after death. (Cox & Parker, 2018, p. 87)

As shown in the previous commentary, the poem expresses passion and an emotional attachment to the addressee. She loves him from all sides and directions. She loves him "freely" as well as "purely", with her mind, soul and entire being. Therefore, the poet does more than disclose and articulate her sensations of love because she scales them down using arcane metaphors and obscure meanings. This leads us to pose the following question: What is meaning?

3.4 Revisiting Meanings

Meaning is what we are trying to capture when we read a text? This is a simple answer to what meaning is, and it is one on which there is general consensus. From there, definitions diverge sharply. Is meaning to be found by attending to the author and his or her intentions? Or is meaning a distinctive property of texts separated from their authors? How do readers intersect with meaning? Do they discover or merely respond to meaning, or are they, in reality, the procreators of meaning? The possible answers we might give to these kinds of questions are, as Brown (2007) notes, more likely to influence our definitions and conceptions of meaning

Based on these common-sense assumptions, where does the true meaning of the poem reside? Is it inside or outside of it? With the constructionist or constructivist approach, meaning is located with the readers because they are also seen as active agents, who can contribute to meaning-making; so, meaning is not what the author intends, but what the reader wants. (Hall, 1997) In truth, when reading the poem, we necessarily interact with the text, by holding an interior monologue about its overall themes and language, and by raising general and text-related queries, and sporadically personal ones that make the poem more meaningful to us. Such queries broaden our scope of the poem and engage us in a deep reflection over its style and underlying message. Our response is, therefore, shaped not only by our experiences but also by our cultural and educational backgrounds.

One crystal meaning that can be easily extracted from the poem at hand is that the speaker is in love with someone – a human being that triggered inspiration and rekindled the power of creativity in the poet to articulate her feelings freely and spontaneously. This love of being with him subsumes three primordial elements: admiration, intellectual interaction and predisposition for marriage and reunion. As well as her tendency for unity, the experimentation of the transcendental is so common to E.B. Browning's writing, which draws on multiple binaries of the earthly and eternal: near and far, higher and lower, temporal and eternal, seen and unseen, internal and external. (Lewis, 2022) The numerous metaphors employed by the poet do not merely embellish the poetic text, but they empower it so as to move the addressee and stir his intimate emotions.

3.5 Types of Metaphors

The speaker dwells on orientational metaphors that are vehicled by her self-projection in various directions to render the love feeling tangible and more perceptible to the average reader. The lexemes designating "locations" like DEPTH, BREADTH, HEIGHT, ENDS, LEVELS, along with those indicating "faith" such as BREATH, SOUL, GRACE, CANDLE- LIGHT, FAITH, SAINTS, GOD reveal that love is a multi-layered concept and that it cannot be captured in words or in verbose expressions.

Ontological metaphors are given due attention by the poet, for they enable the reader to see immaterial phenomena as physical objects." (Haser, 2005) In lines 7-8, for example, the speaker draws an analogy between her loyalty to love and human rights' activists. She unchains herself from the dictations of rigorous orthodoxy, embraces love as a faith, to articulate her heartfelt love – a praiseworthy love that is not tainted by sin or lust in as much as it is akin, in its virtue and splendour, to the mission of noble men: those rising up from praise.

Aside from its emotional innuendoes, the poem dwells on reasoning in the delimitation of love through the counting operation. While the speaker was immersed in substantiating her altruistic love, she found herself incapable of encompassing its totality because love per se is amorphous and indeterminate – always in the process of becoming. What endorses this impressionistic vantage point is the deployment of the uncountable metaphorical nouns such as PASSION [Line 9], LOVE [Line 11], BREATH [Line 12], SMILES and TEARS [Line 13]. These abstractions are pragmatic and purposive because they function as discursive techniques of "the poetic imagination and rhetorical flourish – a matter of extraordinary rather than ordinary language." (Lakoff & Johnson, 1980, p. 453)

The metaphorical reference "I love thee" (n=9) makes the poem anaphoric par excellence. In addition to fostering a persuasive effect, anaphora tends to please the human ears and generate integrity and momentum, so the full-fledged feeling becomes impactful and memorable for many generations to come. In line with Lakoff and Johnson (1980), love can be regarded as a genuine resource for the speaker; it is like fresh air and water -- like money and fortune; hence, different aspects of this non-sensual love are thematized systematically to pinpoint its versatility and cadence.

The most compelling metaphor that E.B. Browning drew on is the metaphor of THE BREATH, which is featured in Line 12. How does it sound to love someone with the breath? Ancient civilizations have equated breath with spirit, divinity and growth, and more precisely, with "a life force." Not only does life start with breath, but it also ends when the same breath comes to a standstill. By casting her love in the realm of the invisible, the intricate domain of THE BREATH, the speaker gives life and continuity to love; hence, the rhythmic flow of love unites her with the addressee with every breath and, if God chooses this love shall prevail even after death. In fact, the term BREATH is so common in poetry, and it inspired several poets. In sonnet 18, William Shakespeare (1564-1616) wrote that whenever men breathe and their eyes see, his writing will last forever, and it will give a new life to his beloved. Rumi has also evoked the idea of BREATH in one of his poems, which is entitled: "Only Breath." He explained that breath always nourishes and sustains the lives of human beings.

In Line 14, the modal verb SHALL, which has a rhetorical tinge too, is emphasized since it expresses the hopeful mood of the speaker and her steady commitment to the faith of love. The epistemic modality at play incorporates not only the preservation but also the perpetuation of the idea of love, which entails that if I LOVE THEE WITH THE BREATH, I SHALL LOVE THEE AFTER DEATH. This entailment can be illustrated in the following diagram:

I		I
LOVE		SHALL
THEE	entails	LOVE
WITH		THEE
THE		AFTER
BREATH		DEATH

Figure 3.1: Entailment in E.B. Browning's "How Do I Love Thee?" (adapted from Lakoff & Johnson, 1980)

Writing a poem about love is expressly a stupendous experience for E.B. Browning; she had to translate faithfully and accurately her deep-seated feelings into words and verse. She had to cloak them with the art of rhetoric and metaphors and inject into them integrity and vigour so that they can do their work on the addressee. These poetic metaphors convey succinct perceptions of love gracefully and economically. In so far as Parsons et al. (1983, p. 442) are concerned, the metaphors of a poem "help the person return ever more deeply to his or her own resources and experience personal wholeness." When metaphors sprout like roses sprouting from a seed, veritable pleasure comes into fruition, and the reader feels engaged and more intrigued. The American essayist, William Styron, has once observed that

> Writing is, of course, work, but it is also a pleasure when it goes well – when ideas feel solid and the writing is fluid. You can experience that pleasure as well, if you approach writing as an intellectual and emotional opportunity rather than merely a sentence. (Meyer, 1996, p. 23)

The poem is, therefore, not just about metaphors but the raw emotions moving the speaker to think and talk freely about human love. In fact, it is these thoroughbred feelings of wish and aspiration, these overflowing thoughts of passion and longing, that made her be at one with her lover to inaugurate together a bond of "sacred love" – an unconditional love that carries humility and truthfulness within, and it tastes like Love itself. With such audacity, she posits love as a mantra – an inclusive faith that contains union as well as unification. Hence, when love is introduced as a faith, cultural differences and geographic boundaries vanish; they discontinue detaching human beings from each other, paving the ground for them to experience peaceful co-existence, mutual harmony and understanding instead of clash or perturbation.

Among the writers who have been inspired enormously by E.B. Browning is the American novelist Nancy Moser (b. 1954), who wrote her novel *How Do I Love Thee?* The novel is classified under inspirational biographical fiction. Throughout the novel, Moser uses Brownings' own words and quotes many passages from their letters. (Moser, 2009) Adams and Neal (2018) have also compiled a picture book building on the iconic famous lines of the poem. Their book sets the example of three friends experiencing a multitude of ways through which love can be felt.

3.6 Conclusion

In this chapter, I have analyzed E.B. Browning's poem, "How Do I Love Thee? Let Me Count The Ways." My critical analysis deployed Lakoff and Johnson's theory of conceptual metaphors", which seems to intersect with rhetoric. The metaphors that were operationalized by the speaker (and the poet) contributed to the initiation of mutual harmony, building proximity and leading to what Ted Cohen had called "the achievement of intimacy." (Hirsch, 1999, p. 15) That is, they allowed the poet to burnish the poetic style and forge a third space of dialogue so as to connect emotionally and intellectually with the addressee. Had these conceptual and rhetorical metaphors been overlooked, the latter would not have accepted her offer and responded more pleasantly. This metaphor analysis applied to the poem differs quite markedly from the linguistic analysis undertaken in the next chapter.

3.7 Further Readings

Browning, E. B., & Browning, R. (2013). *The love letters of Elisabeth Barrett and Robert Browning.* New York: Skyhorse Publishing, Inc.

Carper, T., & Attridge, D. (2002). Scanning poems. *Meter and meaning: An introduction to rhythm in poetry.* New York: Routledge, pp. 46-75.

Jati, A. (2007). Reading up the verse pattern of Elisabeth Barrett Browning's how do I love thee? *TEFLIN journal,* 18(1), pp. 15-25, DOI: http://dx.doi.org/10.15 639/teflinjournal.v18i1/16-27

Pollock, M. S. (2003). *Elisabeth Barrett and Robert Browning: A creative partnership.* London: Routledge.

Reynolds, M. (1997). Love's measurement in Elisabeth Barrett Browning's "sonnets from the Portuguese." *Studies in Browning and his circle,* 21, pp. 53–67. http://www.jstor.org/stable/45285452

3.8 Questions for Discussion

1) Why did the speaker enumerate the ways she loved the addressee?
2) In your opinion, if she framed the title in the declarative form, would it trigger the same impact?
3) Which line has grabbed your full attention? What made you opt for that line?
4) Based on your second reading of the poem, do you think it is easy to talk about concepts such as "love" and "breath" in social settings?
5) How can you characterize the style of the poem? What makes it so?
6) Do you agree that metaphors can contribute to the achievement of closeness and "intimacy"? How?

Chapter 4

A TRANSITIVITY PROCESS ANALYSIS OF "MANNERS"

Highlights:

- *The poem has a didactic tone as it deals with human-appreciated conduct.*
- *E. Bishop has used different clause processes: verbal, mental, material and relational.*
- *The cooperative principle and the four maxims are at stake.*
- *Some character traits such as active listening, communicativeness and empathy are accentuated by the poet.*
- *The use of symbolism is not accidental, for it opens up to various interpretations.*

4.1 Introduction

This chapter, that could be more compelling for students of the Linguistics stream focuses on the application of the Hallidayan model of transitivity on Elisabeth Bishop's (1911-1979) poem, "Manners." Since the poem deals with desirable codes of behaviour, I deem it necessary to start off by talking about poetry's pivotal role in edifying people and its major contribution to their education and self-enlightenment. Besides laying bare the cooperative principle, a wide range of process clauses are identified to showcase some manners that the elderly ought to ingrain in their progeny. Eventually, I explain why objectivity and neutrality remain irksome in any critical reading of and reflection on style.

4.2 The Cooperative Principle

Poetry teaches ethics and it scaffolds people's emotional intelligence to be in coalescence with humanity. Since a poem, as Harrington (2002, p. 28) argues, "teaches [and] edifies", it is identical to the education of citizens because it leads people to emulate characters and incorporate their appreciated behaviour in their social interactions and conversations. Very often, a poem strives for a large public (Von Albrecht, 1997), and it reaches human beings on different levels.

The poem under scrutiny makes us see, hear, feel and even think of the etiquettes required from a child of 1918. Almost in every stanza, the poet instructs character as well as actions to the child, so she can behave with courtesy and kindness in the public sphere. The idea of the public sphere describes all aspects and areas of the human life. It indicates the communicative space frequented by people on a daily basis, who gather together in order to socialize, talk to each other freely and exchange opinions over different matters. It involves strangers and foreigners who met for the first time, for example in public modes of transportation, their interactivity with and attitudes towards other people and species like animals; and it aims to initiate friendship, mutual trust, a peaceful dialogue and harmony between them regardless of their stark differences.

By framing directives in the imperative form, the poet locates the Cooperative Principle (Grice, 1989) in the hands of the grandfather. His lessons appear informative, relevant, factual and poignant. That is, he observed the four Gricean maxims: maxim of quantity (he tries to be informative as much as he can); quality (he tries to be truthful by not giving false information); relation (he says things that are pertinent to the conversation and the education of the child); manner (he tries to be clear, brief, and orderly as much as he can).

At its core, the Cooperative Principle means that in conversation, the speaker does not lie, nor does he/she assume their conversational partners lie – both of them are sincere, and for the most part, they all contribute relevant information. (Denham & Lobeck, 2013) This holds true for the conversation taking place between the grandfather and the child. The way he articulated his words sounded clear and well-organized; hence, the child was not reluctant to put them easily into practice. The lexis employed across the poem relates semantically to the theme of "manners", and the extended clauses underscore the harmonious encounter between two generations, dissimilar mindsets, the things the two participants were involved in, the processes they engaged in and the sort of circumstances in which they occur. (Flowerdew, 2013)

Contextual parameters such as field, tenor, mode, along with their corresponding lexico-grammatical choices allow the poem to impart salient and vivid meanings to the reader, each of which generates interest in good manners. The child follows her grandfather's advice verbatim with no reluctance or hesitation: "I said it" / "bowed where I sat." The field is established in the title, which "indicates its focus." (Langdell, 2018, p. 94) Tenor evinces in the participants: the grandfather, an expert providing wisdom and edification, and his child, being a novice recipient of advice and knowledge. The mode, however, is created by virtue of commands which appertain to informal spoken language. In order that students could identify easily the types of processes included in the poem, I suggest that they focus on the main verbs included either by circling or underlining them and then categorize these verbs according to their respective functions.

4.3 Types of Process Clauses

The verbal process clauses (n=5) indicate the grandfather's aim to enhance the education and social skills of the child. These clauses designate the processes of saying, which is realized by the verb "said" (n=4). As for the participants, they are as follows: the Sayer, Receiver and Verbiage. The Sayer alludes to the addresser, the Receiver indicates the addressee, whereas the Verbiage refers to the content of the message. Verbal process clauses, according to Halliday (2004), contribute to the creation of narratives by setting up distinctive dialogues and reported speech. Table 4.1 illustrates the verbal process clauses that figure in the entire poem. Most of the time, it is the grandfather who initiates the verbiage since he is old, wise and more experienced than the child:

Table 4.1: Verbal Process Clauses

Sayer	Verbal Process	Receiver	Verbiage	Circumstance
My grandfather	said	me	Be sure to speak to everyone you meet	
I	said		it	
My grandfather	said		Always offer ... get older	
My grandfather	said		A fine bird And he is well brought up...do	
We	shouted		Good day! Good day! Fine day	at the top of our voices

Mental processes (n=4) are not overlooked, for the intent of the speaker is not just to think about manners but to take good actions, as we shall see. These processes have to do with memory, thinking and imagination, and more precisely, with the things that go on in the mind of the child. The mental process verbs that fall within this rubric are "feel", "see", "think", "believe", "want", "like", yet in the poem, they are realized only by three cognitive verbs: "overtake", "forget" and "know." The tense choice for these processes is the simple present and past. In addition to the verb, mental process clauses contain two participants: the Senser (someone who senses) and the Phenomenon (something that is sensed). Table 4.2 presents the major mental process clauses of the poem. Sometimes the Senser is realized by the pronoun "We" and at other times by "He"; whereas, the Phenomenon is virtually absent or is an implied "you". As for the circumstance (time, place, manner, etc.), the speaker resorts to spatio-temporal deixis to develop her theme around the virtues and blessings of good manners:

Table 4.2: Mental Process Clauses

Senser	Mental Process	Phenomenon	Circumstance
We	overtook	a boy	with his big pet
	don't forget		when you get older
We	knew		
He	know		where to go

Interestingly, one can note that material process clauses (n=13) outnumber other process clauses. One reason for the privileging of the material over the mental is that the speaker is not fixed in her place, but she is moving from one social setting to another. That is, she is being taught specific codes of behaviour in real-life situations with the view to becoming empathic, kind-hearted and more considerate.

Character traits like effective communication, active listening, empathy and benevolence, open-mindedness, can all be extrapolated from E. Bishop's poem. These character traits are cloaked in the material process clauses, which involve verbs of doing and motion; they have an Actor (the doer / the one who performs the action) and a Goal (that to which / to whom something is done), and periodically a Circumstance. Of particular note here is the preponderance of the Actor "We" (n=4) that not only alludes to the grandfather and the child but also to their uniformity and conformity with the aforementioned character traits. Table 4.3 encapsulates the material process clauses, whose Goal features as a person, an inanimate object or an animal:

Table 4.3: Material Process Clauses

Actor	Material Process	Goal	Circumstance
We	sat		on the wagon seat
We	met	a stranger	on foot
My grandfather's whip	tapped	his hat	
	bowed		where I sat
Willy	climbed up	us	
The crow	gave	a caw	
	flew off		
Willy	whistled		
Automobiles	went by		
The dust	hid	the people	
We	came		to Hustler Hill
We	got down		
	walked		

Whereas material process clauses involve dynamic / action verbs, relational process clauses (n=3) involve static ones; they tend to ascribe an attribute to an entity (Note, for example, "worried", "well-brought up", "tired"), yet they have been subordinated because the poet's purpose is to upgrade the child's demeanor to observe acumen and courtesy. Such processes "serve to characterize and to identify" (Halliday, 2004, p. 210) humans and other species like animals. In our case, they are facilitated by the verb "to be" that denotes being and existing. The participants in relational process clauses depend on whether the relational process clause is identifying or attributive. The obligatory participant in attributive relational process clauses is the Carrier, which comes before the verb. The latter is followed by an Attribute, which may be an adjectival or nominal group. (Flowerdew, 2013)

As Table 4.4 demonstrates, the child was described as being worried only once, when she saw the crow giving a "Cawl" and flying off. That the latter answers nicely the calls when spoken to reveals that good manners are not exclusive to human beings as they can englobe living creatures such as companion or pet animals. Such creatures can be responsive and friendly because they are more likely to impart warmth and shelter to people in critical times. Not only can they delight in the presence of strangers, but they can sustain sickness and physical fatigue as well. Consider Table 4.4, which represents the relational process clauses of the poem:

Table 4.4: Relational Process Clauses

Carrier	Relational Process	Attribute
I	was	worried
He	is	well-brought up
The mare	was	tired

As a result, the metaphor of the crow and the mare are not arbitrary since they have a profound meaning, which adds another dimension to the interpretation. (Halliday & Matthiessen, 2006) If the crow symbolizes metamorphosis and intelligence, the mare incarnates "the attitude that the noble man must adopt." (Lim, 2000, p. 119) The interpretation accorded to the metaphorical meanings of the poem might sound a little subjective, but it is complementary to literal meanings that sometimes do not do justice to poetry.

4.4 Objectivity vs. Subjectivity

This transitivity approach to style that I implemented on Bishop's poem, "Manners", borrows some theoretical insights from Halliday's leading work on Systemic Functional Grammar (SFG). It is one model of analysis that strives hard to achieve objectivity and neutrality because it distances itself from impressionistic readings of texts. By objectivity, I mean that the technical terminology used, instruments, and tools of analysis, should be both transparent and common so that other researchers can verify their credibility and validity. (Simpson, 2004) The stylistic analysis can be objective when it is free of personal opinions and impressions, biases and value judgments yet objectivity and neutrality, as two contested concepts, are occasionally hard to achieve. (Holloway & Galvin, 2010; Brundrett & Rhodes, 2014)

It is true that some levels of language, such as phonology and phonetics, together with syntax and morphology, are the major arenas where the stylistic analysis can stand objective and unbiased; however, when certain methods are included and others excluded, the stylistic analysis ceases to be purely objective. For example, do researchers need to study style qualitatively or quantitatively? Is it sufficient to address just the phonological or morphological traits of style? Is it compulsory to examine the syntactic and graphological aspects? And if the answer is a big "No", would it be rather pertinent to adopt a multi-faceted perspective – a hodge-podge of utensils from all the fields and sub-fields of language. When style is approached at the level of pragmatics and discourse analysis, the stylistic analysis becomes somewhat impressionistic and subjective. This happens because the meanings deducted and interpretations arrived at are not independent of one's background knowledge, people's moral preferences, their cultures, beliefs, and gender. These elements, arguably, affect the perception of style and its appreciation. My belief is that the questions of objectivity and subjectivity will keep annoying explorers of meaning and investigators of style for many years to come.

The transitivity model of analysis presented has moved from the description of the major clauses to the interpretation of meaning and metaphors. Such microscopic reading of style is beneficial because it can explain, on the one hand, the complex roles of participants, their relations, and how they are projected in a given clause; and on the other hand, it can hone students' thinking abilities and writing skills. It is relevant to the study of poetry as it will raise students' awareness of language and open up their eyes to the notion of power and ideology in the realm of discourse.

4.5 Conclusion

In this chapter, I have applied Halliday's theory of transitivity to E. Bishop's poem, "Manners" in as much as this approach makes the stylistic analysis accurate, retrievable and falsifiable. The Cooperative Principle, including the four maxims, is juxtaposed with four clause processes in order to enable the reader to constitute a clear view about ancient proper manners and reflect on their implementation in their quotidian lives. Last but not least, the questions of objectivity and subjectivity are stressed out to help researchers pay attention to them in their critical readings of and responses to poetic style. The upcoming chapter presents a resistant reading to Yeat's short poem, "Memory."

4.6 Further Readings

Furlani, A. (2020). Elizabeth Bishop's animal manners, *Essays in criticism*, 70 (4), pp. 428– 446, https://doi.org/10.1093/escrit/cgaa024

Goldensohn, L. (1992). *Elisabeth Bishop: The biography of a poetry*. New York: Columbia U Press.

Harrison, V. (1993). *Elisabeth Bishop's poetics of intimacy*. New York: Cambridge U Press.

Logan, W. (1994). The unbearable lightness of Elizabeth Bishop. *Southwest review*, 79(1), pp. 120–138, http://www.jstor.org/stable/43470544

Millier, B. C. (1995). *Elisabeth Bishop: Life and the memory of it*. Oxford: U of California Press, Ltd.

4.7 Questions for Discussion

1) What is transitivity? How does it operate in SFG?

2) In your opinion, why should students familiarize themselves with such approach to style?

3) In what way does transitivity analysis relate to the dichotomy of style and discourse?

4) Which types of process clauses were not considered by E. Bishop in her poem, "Manners"? Why did she exclude them?

5) Why did the poet draw on the symbols of the mare and the crow? If these animals were not included in the poem, how would the poem sound to you?

6) Can you think of other animals that poets have built on to express their feelings and transmit their messages to their audience?

Chapter 5

AN ABERRANT DECODING OF "MEMORY"

Highlights:

- *People tend to relate beauty and face to physicality.*
- *Meanings are both denotative and connotative.*
- *The reader can propose another reading of the text on account of his/her background knowledge.*
- *The dominant code sometimes limits understanding and interpretation.*
- *Umberto Eco's aberrant reading can uncover another facet of style and discourse.*

5.1 Introduction

This chapter is designed to cater to the needs of students of Stylistics and Pragmatics; it is an explication of the notion of beauty as portrayed in William Butler Yeats' (1865-1939) poem, "Memory." Following Barthes' (1967) denotative and connotative meanings and Umberto Eco's (1972) concept of "Aberrant Decoding" (in Italian: *decodifica aberrante*), I explain why beauty cannot be dissociated from the concept of face and memory. Since the poem is short, we can analyze it line by line. (Jeffries & McIntyre, 2010) First, let us see how the notion of beauty was conceived in Greek thought and philosophy.

5.2 Approaching Beauty

Beauty has always been associated with physicality and the human face; it is viewed as a force that enlightens humanity since it is so capable of restoring life to its existence and ensuring its continuity. Two patterns of beauty impose themselves in the vast world: one is seen, and the other is unseen, yet the gurus of philosophical sapience will not disagree that beauty dwells in the eyes of the beholder.

In the most general terms, beauty could indicate the characteristics of a human being, object, place, time, or idea that imparts a perceptual experience of pleasure, meaning and satisfaction. However, in its most profound sense, beauty tends to generate a remarkable experience of positive reflection about the meaning of people's own existence. Thus, the experience of beauty necessitates the accentuation of positive elements and the incorporation of balance and harmony with nature, as this harmony can lead to feelings of emotional well-being (Desmond, 2011) and allows for sublimity and perfection to come full-fledged.

For many Greek philosophers, beauty included a concept of the soul and virtue. Plato and Aristotle have attached it to ethics, good health and youth, and it is more than surface alone. (Harris-Moore, 2014) In his dialogue with Socrates, Hippias declared: "I am certain that what I said is beautiful to everyone – nobody will deny that!" Socrates replied: "Will it be beautiful in the future as well, because beauty is always beautiful." (Anderson, 2007, p. 13) This answer implies that beauty, aside from being associated with people's individual tastes and perceptions, is characterized by being immortal and perennial.

How does beauty stand in "Memory"? As we shall see, W.B. Yeats has linked beauty to face. The term "face" here is contested as it does not necessarily point to a part of the human body because it can be regarded as an abstract notion and appellation. Brown and Levinson (1987), for example, posit that 'face' is the socially given self-image consisting of positive and negative face. Negative face refers to the desire not to be obstructed by others, while positive face refers to the desire to be accepted by others. Like any other term, "face" can be approached in a denotative and connotative way.

5.3 Denotation and Connotation

According to Branston and Stafford (2010), signs not only signify and name, but they also *denote* different aspects of our experience or of the world. Take, for instance, the term "red", it denotes one part of the colour spectrum, distinguished from other parts such as "green" or "black" within what is, in fact, a continuous spectrum, with colours merging with one another. But signs also *connote*, or link things. They may bind things by repeated association with broader cultural concepts and values, as well as with meanings from personal history and experience. This debate, which tends to draw clear boundaries between denotation and connotation is not new. Valli and Lucas (2000) have dubbed the referential meaning of a sign or a sentence "denotation", while the social and affective meaning has been described by them as "connotation."

When examining myth, the French literary theorist and semiotician, Roland Barthes (1915-1980), has talked about "denotated meaning" (or denotation) for first-order meaning, and "connotated meaning" (or connotation) for second-order meaning. Either concept is now widely deployed to examine all sorts of messages – be they a poem or otherwise. The main difference between the two terms, as Ribière (2008) argues, is that

> [D]enotation, or first-order meaning, is stable – a haircut is always a haircut. Whereas connotation, or second-order meaning, depends on context. In a different situation, and/or at a different time, a haircut similar to that of Abbé Pierre's could be perceived, for example, as a daring hairstyle, and therefore connote not "humility", but "arrogance."

When reading "Memory", the reader notices that words generate not only meanings but feelings as well. These feelings live within a wider world of context and interpretation, both of which make the poem alive, rich and not dead at all.

5.4 Context

In poetry, context is considered as a core notion because it is helpful in the clarification of meaning, and it is viewed as a key factor in effective reading and interpretation. The context of "Memory" subsumes not only the production of the text but its reception as well; it involves the tempo-spatial circumstances in or at which it was produced. Observes Mey (2001, p. 41), "Context is more than just reference. Context is action. Context is about understanding what things are for; it is also what gives our utterances their true pragmatic meaning and allows them to be counted as true pragmatic acts."

Following the same stream of thought, Van Dijk (2006) has proposed that contexts are not 'objective' or 'deterministic' constraints of society or culture at all, but subjective participant interpretations, constructions or definitions of such aspects of the social environment. From what we know about the poem in our minds, such 'definitions' are mental, and in many situations they are only mental, and not expressed or formulated in discourse, although they may influence discourse. When bringing context into action, Yeats' poem "Memory" becomes a discourse and not just a static text, for its interpretation is influenced enormously by the authorial and socio-historical contexts, the reader's worldviews, their cultures, beliefs and gender backgrounds. Hence, each one of them will peel the poem according to their mind frames, psyche and emotional awareness. By emotional awareness, I mean the reader's ability to understand and recognize not only their emotions but also the emotions of the poet as expressed in words and verse. The critical analysis structured below considers the entire lines of the poem, and in the meantime, it retains the opening owing to the voluble brevity and conciseness of the text.

5.5 Peeling the Skin of the Poem

5.5.1 One ... [Line 1]

In a witty and rhetorical style, Yeats commences his compact poem "Memory" with the indefinite pronoun "one", which is striking and eye-catching for the reader because it might indicate any person or individual. It seems that Yeats has spent much time searching for a neutral, unprejudiced -- a singular personal pronoun and could not find a better solution than "this general-type allusion" that sometimes operates as a generic inclusiveness, for it is useful in some scenarios where one or more people fit into a given action, occasion, or state of being. (Jarrad, 2012) By screening the face as "lovely", Yeats wants to evoke the image of delightfulness and adorability. Denotatively, the term yields these meanings: pretty, gorgeous, charming, handsome, good-looking, attractive, beautiful, and the list goes on and on. Connotatively, it betrays the imprint faces leave on onlookers and passersby from the first sight. A lovely face means a lovely soul and a good heart. Very often, lovely people are friendly, cordial, outgoing, amiable, and it is always pleasurable to listen to or look at them.

Writing about faces was a common practice for ancient poets. John Dryden (1631-1700), for instance, wrote that a person can charm him not with that fair face. Emily Dickinson (1830-1886) noted that a charm invests a face. Charles Lamb (1775-1834) told us about the old familiar faces; conversely, Gibran Khalil Gibran (1883-1931) wrote simply: "Faces." That poets take face and charm as their subjects of study demonstrate that faces are not really in vain. One poem that I found so compelling about face and charm is entitled, "Looking For Your Face"; it was drafted in the thirteenth century by the mystical poet Rumi (1207-1273), who unravelled his longing for his master's dazzling beauty and spiritual insights, vehicling his penchant for his enlightened face in a marvellous way, to the extent that he becomes one with it. Rumi stated that he has been looking for that face since the beginning of his life; and today he was fortunate because he can see it, and he can see the charm, the unfathomable grace of the face he was looking for.

5.5.2 And ... [Line 2]

In the second line, Yeats proceeds on an unbiased talk by evoking the coordinating conjunction "and" as well as the counting numbers "two" or "three." The first is used to join the first two independent lines that apparently have equal importance; nevertheless, the second is used not only to specify how many people had charm but also to make the talk flow quite smoothly. Again, Yeats solicits sophistication and creativity in terms of style and poetic expressions when he stopped at number "three." Although this cardinal number is suggestive of trinity in the Christian orthodoxy, it is included to reinforce the idea of multiplicity as concerns charm and face. The counting process has enabled Yeats to stand in person as an observer, and to use Gordon's (1998) words, he is akin to a photographer; he does with words what the photographer does with a camera.

On turning to "charm", Yeats releases himself of the manacles of corporeality and the visual to access the mysteries of beauty and face and unveil how they move people; how they bewitch them, and most important of all, how they trigger admiration, fascination and bewilderment in street onlookers and passersby. He pinpoints that "charm" is useless and in vain. However, when truth and good come into play, as Tagore (1861-1941) observes, charm regains another signification, and the beautiful stands revealed. (qtd. in Ray, 2018) Charm is, of course, not the same as beauty, but it is a subdivision of it. (Benson, 2019) Sometimes, it is seen as far more captivating and affecting than beauty.

5.5.3 But ... [Line 3]

The endorsement of "this preferred reading", as Hall (1973) hails it, expresses the speaker's discontent with the magic of outer charm [Line 3]. The ordering of words is purposeful since the first gives rise to the second; indeed, the two function as a leitmotif to consolidate the claim that beauty itself is ephemeral and that such ephemerality brings forth both despair and disillusionment. Yeats was successful in gearing the reader to an unusual emotion emanating from the evanescence of beauty and charm. The imposed meaning, so to speak, is exclusive of the vital role of the reader in the interpretation of the text The term text here designates the poet's sophisticated thoughts and ideas and his perception of abstract nouns such as beauty and charm.

5.5.4 Because ... [Line 4]

The move towards natural elements like "the mountain grass" [Line 4] is inherent in romantic poetry that thrived in the romantic era. This poetry engages an intimacy with natural spaces deemed as "living things" that inspire poets. Literally, the image of "the mountain grass" indicates a large steep hill of the earth full of grass. Metaphorically, it alludes to the human body that hosts corporeal beauty as represented in charm and face. It is a marker of and vehicle for life, recollection and ingenuity. After all, the adverbial clause of cause fronted at the beginning of the fourth line assigns both reason and cause to help warrant the subjectivity of the speaker's view. In congruency with Hall (1973), the dominant code positions the readers, limits and controls their interpretation. This is why aberrant decoding provides a good alternative since it does not kill the text but keeps it moving and evolving.

5.5.5 Cannot ... [Line 5]

The emphasis, deployed in the fifth line, through the prism of negative modality is intended to grab the readers' attention and provoke their thoughts. The physical form does not last forever, and it becomes decadent over time. This holds true for the grass as it does not preserve its original form and colour; it withers up and turns like a straw, especially in summer. What Yeats obscures is the location where lasting beauty and face reside; it can be the realm of the heart, or to borrow a phrase from the American philosopher and essayist, Ralph Waldo Emerson (1803-1882), the "Over-Soul" (see Atkinson, 1940). No wonder then that Yeats stirs up the readers' minds to search for them in this alley of metaphors and allegorical images, paving the ground for them to use their cognition and schemata appropriately. The feeling obscured, no matter how joyful or melancholic it might be, stimulates one to read and re-read the poem several times.

5.5.6 Where ... [Line 6]

It is in the last line [Line 6] that Yeats introduces one character, "the hare" – a tiny creature with numerous symbolisms in English literature. Lumpkin and Seidensticker (2011) argue that hares are usually indicative of timidity and fearfulness. Hares have been so common in the visual arts, and human literature abounds with them. Most of the time, they have been associated with the moon deities, and they could also be signifiers of resurrection and rebirth. Thus, "the mountain hare" might refer to a human beauty that the speaker has spotted, loved and even embraced, yet the emotional attachment to it, or his soulful connection to it, might have come to a standstill point. When we consider the mountain and the speediness of this little creature in the woods, it becomes clear that physical beauty is fleeting like "the hare" and nothing remains excepting ashes and memory.

5.6 Conclusion

The above stylistic analysis does not align with the dominant voice of the poetic text; on the contrary, it resists it by tapping on other meanings of face and beauty. To cut it short, before one can interpret or discuss a short poem, as Kennedy and Gioia note (1995), one will have to read it slowly and painstakingly, with their minds open and ready. As dreams constitute a big part of human life, I deem it necessary to expose the reader in the next chapter to Afro-American dreams using insights from the constructivist approach, which seems to overlap with aberrant decoding.

5.7 Further Readings

Finneran, R. J. (Ed.). (1996). *Collected poems of W.B. Yeats*. New York: Macmillan Publishing Company.

Love, T. (2012). "Memory" by W.B. Yeats, http://litrefsarticles.blogspot.com/2012/06/memory-by-wb-yeats.html

Prestwich, E. (2011). W.B Yeats: "Memory", https://edmundprestwich.co.uk/?p=522

Ross, D. A. (2009) *Critical companion to William Butler Yeats: A literary reference to his life and work*. New York: Facts On File, Inc.

Widdowson, H. G. (1992). *Practical stylistics: An approach to poetry*. New York: Oxford.

5.8 Questions for Discussion

1) What are the major themes that you can extrapolate from W.B. Yeats' poem "Memory"?
2) In your opinion, why did the poet choose to focus on those themes?
3) Is there any difference between denotative and connotative meaning? Can you provide examples to illustrate your point?
4) How does the preferred reading work?
5) Can you cite some poets who have raised the concept of beauty and face in their poetry?
6) Reformulate the poem in your own style and focus on "Beauty"; "Face"; "Lovely"; "Charm." How can you describe the experience of poetry writing?

Chapter 6

AFRO-AMERICAN "DREAMS": A CONSTRUCTIVIST APPROACH

Highlights:

- *Dreams is a theme that is recurrent in African American literature*
- *They indicate short, medium and long-term goals that people, oppressed or unoppressed, can attain.*
- *Readers ought to adopt a constructivist reading approach to fathom the substance of Afro-American dreams.*
- *Bakhtin's notion of dialogism ensures that there is a strong connection between Hughes' poem "Dreams" and Martin Luther King's speech "I Have a Dream."*
- *Dreams prompt human beings to act positively, attentively and more consciously.*

6.1 Introduction

This chapter explores the Afro-American dream that found an enormous space in the writings of Langston Hughes (1901-1967), Martin Luther King, Jr. (1929-1968), and others. By disambiguating the notion of dreams, I endeavour to expose students of Literary and Rhetoric Studies to analogical thinking by putting forth the hopes of people of colour, who constantly struggle to achieve equality and lead a successful narrative alongside their white compatriots. Bakhtin's (1984) concept of "dialogism", Deleuze (1983) view of "minor literature", are considered since they can help the prospective reader to build a holistic view of the Afro-American dream and discern why it is recurrent in Afro-American literature.

6.2 A Dream Deferred

Dreams have been the most compelling theme for the African American poets and writers. They have brought about a major breakthrough in their literary inspiration and masterly canon. Functioning like a "divine flashlight" (Martins, 2012) and "creativity catalysts" (Packer, 2002), dreams have enlightened the way ahead of them and allowed them to pursue paths of change, so they can face life's predicaments with hope and efficacy. Occasionally, these dreams have been misunderstood and undefined, yet at their heart lies an essential sustaining quality. (Scott, 2002) The quality of seeking esteem, racial equality and recognition, either through expressions of hope or feelings of despair, resonates across Afro- American literature.

African American poets and writers have found, as Mallon (2002, p. 99) posits, "a rich vein of material in their dreams." Langston Hughes is undoubtedly one of those African American poets and writers who had cherished and marvelled at the blessings of dreams in his poetry because he urged people to hold fast to them in order that they could lead a life of success and prosperity. His mellifluous poem, "Dreams", originally published by *The World Tomorrow* magazine in 1923, besides corroborating the spirit of hope and triggering the ethos of communality and efflorescence, reveals to readers "how not holding onto our dreams could adversely affect our qualities as human beings." (Brown, 2013, p. 5) But what sort of dreams does the Harlem Renaissance poet concern himself with? Despite the stark opacity encapsulating this contested space he consistently and so eloquently painted in verse, Hughes' dreams constitute a mysterious realm for the readers to explore and experience. His dreams are camouflaged as "cognitive events" (Mackey, 1985) ensuring to a large extent the social welfare and well-being of his compatriots and reassuring them that only their dreams can unlock new horizons for their future because they have the capacity to provide direction, insight and innovation. (Gonzales, 2012)

An initial reading of his poem demonstrates that the speaker encourages everyone to adhere to dreams, big or small, and to bear the outcomes in case such dreams forsake their everyday lives. Without an optimistic mindset, a hopeful attitude and a steady resolution, the status quo appears infertile and static, the metaphors of which the "broken-winged bird" and the "barren field" expressly indicate. (Pöhlmann, 2015) The focalization of dreams in Hughes's poem then underscores that the human life gains its significance when dreams are maintained and when they last forever. In so far as Steven Tracy is concerned,

> Dreams have always figured prominently in the works of Langston Hughes. Hughes' work is devoted to outlining, celebrating, and agitating on behalf of the dreams of oppressed and marginalized peoples worldwide, with particular focus on the dreams of African Americans. (Tracy, 2002, p. 223)

Arguably, the dreams that Hughes wrote about are short, medium and long-term goals that are more likely to energize outgroups both intrinsically and extrinsically to claim their unswerving rights as humans. They are goals that appear to be in the distant future and challenging to attain. Although those dreams should be realistic, they also need to demonstrate a high degree of confidence in people's ability to work toward achieving them. (Etnier, 2009) The goals, and to use Hughes' words, can be described as "A dream deferred" (Hughes, 1958, p. 123) that can reinvigorate as well as sustain vulnerable people's day-to-day societal practices and behaviours. When these goals are lost, life, at least from Hughes' vantage point, becomes non-sensical and of no avail. Hence, Hughes subsumes into his poem a goal-setting approach, which renders the poem more meaningful and engaging for the contemporary readers since it functions as an antidote to their occasional meltdowns and a springboard for their growth and achievements, fueling their personal life with positive energy and vigour.

6.3 Unpacking Hughes' Dreams

To unpack the enigma and obscurity permeating Hughes' introspections on dreams, readers are entailed to adopt a constructivist reading approach by surveying and pondering upon Martin Luther King's (1929-1968) speech, "I Have a Dream", which reads more as "oral poetry" (Alvarez, 1988) than prose owing to the abundance of poetic expressions, imagery and metaphors. In this memorable speech, Martin Luther King voiced out his desire for peace and racial harmony (Washington, 2015), and he "struggled to restore unity (Fairclough, 1995), freedom and equality in the United States thanks to his firm belief in dreams. As he declared at the March on Washington in 1963:

> I have a dream that one day this nation will rise up and live out the true meaning of its creed: "We hold these truths to be self-evident, that all men are created equal." I have a dream that one day on the red hills of Georgia, the sons of former slaves and the sons of former slave owners will be able to sit down together at the table of brotherhood (...). I have a dream that my four little children will one day live in a nation where they will not be judged by the color of their skin but by the content of their character. (qtd. in Sandquist, 2009, p. 232)

The speech was momentous both because it touched all the themes of the day and because it was full of the symbolism of Lincoln and Ghandi, and the cadences of the Bible. (Reston, 1963) The sad innuendoes of the speech re-echo the feelings of sorrow and depression, which Hughes overshadowed through the two metaphors and signed expressions. The texts, albeit differing quite markedly in form and content, could be exploited as a terrain for the exploration of the African American dream that thrilled numerous poets and writers since time immemorial.

The robust link built horizontally between the poem and the rhetorical speech evinces not only in the presence of repetitions and anaphora but also in the writers' investment in intertextuality and dialogism. In fact, both writers have embellished their literary pieces with the same foregrounding patterns; they accentuated the unending wonders of dreams and their substantive importance to humanity and African American communities in particular. Whereas, Martin Luther King has singularized his dream at times by the usage of the first- person pronoun "I" and at other times by the editorial "we", Langston Hughes opted for the pluralization of his dreams, taking advantage of commands cloaked in the imperative and a vague pronoun reference.

6.4 Dialogism and Intertextuality

Such overt interaction between Langston Hughes' "Dreams" and Martin Luther King Speech "I Have a Dream" showcases that the meaning of dreams is not embedded in the word dreams itself, but it is made salient in this interactive dialogue between writers and readers or between texts and their historical contexts. Mikhail Bakhtin appears quite pertinent in the explication of the African American dreams because he assumed that any piece of writing involves multiple voices (polyphony) and traces of other texts (intertextuality).

Based on the assumption that poets and writers serve as mouthpieces for their communities, I argue that Langston Hughes and Martin Luther King have indexed the voices of the masses into their own and amalgamated their own perspectives to be homogeneous with the perspectives of their readers and viewers. Thus, the dreams that emerged in their texts are not created of one single consciousness but of several patterns of consciousness. In this regard, Mikhail Bakhtin proclaims:

> [T]his interaction provides no support for the viewer who would objectify an entire event according to some ordinary monologic category (thematically, lyrically or cognitively) – and this consequently makes the viewer also a participant. (Bakhtin, 1984, p. 18)

He further adds, "Two voices is the minimum for life, the minimum for existence (ibid., p. 252). The voices of vulnerable communities, along with their aspirations for acceptability, respectability and dignity can be extrapolated from the dreams endorsed by the African American poets and writers. Their dreams comprise the hopes, the expectations and grand ambitions that these communities and outgroups aim to realize in their social environments. They are, according to Hart (2016, p. 326), "driven by conscious and unconscious motivations, and they are indicative of an individual or group's commitments towards a particular trajectory or end point." Be it as it may, African American dreams are dynamic, interconnected, overlapping with the dreams of other minorities, and they tend to be associated with the longed-for "success-stories" (Helin et al., 2022), yet they have been periodically thwarted by racism and xenophobia. They are dreams of a promised land where men and women of all cultures, belief systems and races can live together peacefully with no segregation or discrimination.

> It is not a dream of motor cars and high wages merely, but a dream of a social order in which each man and each woman shall be able to attain to the fullest stature of which they are innately capable, and be recognized by others for what they are, regardless of the fortuitous circumstances of birth or position. (Adams, 1931, p. 404)

Treading on Langston Hughes and Martin Luther King's footsteps are the following African American writers and poets, who have capitalized on and cleverly exploited the theme of dreams as their muse of inspiration since they enthused over developing and discussing it in their works using a wide range of images and symbols. Maya Angelou's (1928-2014) "Still I Rise", Alice Walker's (b. 1944) "Desire", Lucille Clifton's (1936-2010) "Won't You Celebrate With Me", Paul Laurence Dunbar's (1872-1906) "Sympathy", and Nikki Giovanni's (b. 1943) "Dreams", to mention but a handful, are all poems that strive hard for combating racism, oppression and uprooting all forms of violence – direct and structural, or even cultural (Galtung, 1990) These poems relate to minority writing and minor literature where "everything in them is political." (Deleuze, 1983, p. 16) They lean towards empowering marginalized groups like people of colour, for they castigated the consumed stereotypes depicting them as innately lazy, uneducated, less intelligent and less patriotic than whites. (Lipsitz, 2006) One question that arises here is as follows: How do African American writers and poets visualize their future?

6.5 Visions of a Brighter Future

Dreams paved the ground for Afro-American poets and writers to transcend the present, and they supported them to challenge the status quo by campaigning for and hankering after a better and brighter future. Their dreams are presumably compatible with the American dream narrative as reflected in the wish for comfort, cohabitation, equity and the accomplishment of human lower and higher needs. (Maslow, 1943) The fulfilment of these needs remains contingent upon the opportunities looming up for the African American communities, their individual figments and wishes. As Freud (1900, p. 567) observes, "[n]othing but a wish can set our mental apparatus working."

Probably what Langston Hughes and Martin Luther King were driving at was the activation of that mental apparatus to emotionally move the people of colour and bring them on an equal footing with the white majorities; hence, they urged their counterparts to embrace optimism and to behave positively, attentively and more consciously (Morosini, 2010) in order to reach their goals and accomplish their pre-eminent dreams. As a voice speaking on behalf of their people, these two writers have unleashed their imagination and turned their aspirations into a collective reality. If students are capable of responding to their dreams as writers would wish them to do, they must eventually make the same discovery as these writers themselves. (Cluysenaar, 1976)

6.6 Conclusion

This chapter has studied goal-setting and dialogism in Afro-American poetry. More precisely, it demonstrated why Afro-American writers and poets delighted in the articulation of dreams in their creative literary productions and how they call upon other minorities (i.e., people of colour) to share their wishes and dreams for the espousal of equality in their social milieu. Langston Hughes and Martin Luther King have been brought together to allow the readers to approach their texts critically and creatively and to regard these texts as two inseparable entities conveying one homogeneous doctrine and a uniform voice. As they can be active contributors to meaning-making like writers, readers, namely students' sense of creativity is focalized in the next chapter, which deals with reader-response theory and Walter D. Wintle's poem, "Thinking."

6.7 Further Readings

Dualé, C. (2018). Langston Hughes's poetic vision of the American dream: A complex and creative encoded language. *Angles: New perspectives on the Anglophone world*, 7, https://doi.org/10.4000/angles.920

Miller, R. B. (2006). *The art and imagination of Langston Hughes*. Lexington, KY: The U Press of Kentucky.

Sargent, L. T. (2020). African Americans and Utopia: Visions of a better life. *Utopian studies*, 31 (1), pp. 25-96, https://doi.org/10.5325/utopianstudies.31.1.0025

Wallace, M. (2008). *Langston Hughes: The Harlem renaissance*. New York: Marshall Cavendish.

Wei, X. (2007). Use of dreams in Hughes's poetry. *Canadian social science*, 3 (5), pp. 128- 131, http://dx.doi.org/10.3968/j.css.1923669720070305.024

6.8 Questions for Discussion

1) Why did the poet compare dreams to "a broken bird that cannot fly"?

2) In your opinion, which incentives prompted the poet to speak and write about dreams?
3) How can you describe the style of the poem?
4) Are there any similarities / differences between "Dreams" and "Memory"?
5) Do you agree that multiple voices are included in the poem? Think of adequate arguments to back up your claim.

Chapter 7

READER-RESPONSE THEORY: EXPLORING STUDENTS' SENSE OF CREATIVITY

> **Highlights:**
>
> - *Unlike New Criticism, reader-response theory encourages readers to bring their experiences and beliefs to the world of the text.*
> - *The text has no existence unless read and interpreted in a creative way by students.*
> - *Any poem that inspires them to think positively is deemed motivational.*
> - *Positive talk helps diminish students' fear and anxiety when they feel overwhelmed by university courses.*
> - *Teachers need to find suitable links between reading and writing.*

7.1 Introduction

One of the theories that sparked the interest of modern scholars is reader-response theory, which is widely known as reader-response criticism. This theory, while it sheds light on the act of reading, especially in terms of the many ways in which readers react to literary texts, emphasizes the idea that meaning is fluid and evolving by its very nature. This chapter, which could appeal to students of literary criticism and creative writing, traces the historical evolution of reader-response theory and explains why such theory is becoming a must in the reception of literature, mainly motivational poetry. By appropriating Louise Rosenblatt's concept of "selective attention", I intend to explore undergraduate students' sense of creativity in the reception of and reaction to Walter D. Wintle's poem, "Thinking." The next questions are the focus of my investigation:

Q1. Do students' critical reactions to the aforementioned poem reiterate the same textual meanings as intended by the poet, or do they come up with their own distinctive (reader) meanings?
Q2. Can the poem cherish a multitude of interpretations and meanings commensurate with the number of students?
Q3. Which pronouns have been foregrounded by the student-readers to situate themselves in the world of the poem?

7.2 Historical Synopsis

Reader-response criticism is a critical school of thought that lays much emphasis on the fundamental role of readers and their critical reflections on literary works as opposed to ancient theories that privilege the supremacy of the author and the autonomy of the text in the apprehension of meaning. The reflections afforded by this theory are presumably very rewarding both for teachers and their students. Not only does reader-response theory encourage multiple interpretations of texts, but it also prompts students to engage in classroom discussions and consequently display self-autonomy and a great interest. They can articulate their viewpoints freely without being suffocated by the intricacy of the restrictions imposed by pure New Criticism or any Formalist models of analysis.

Admittedly, reader-response criticism is becoming an engaging field in literary studies and second language learning since it provides teachers with an insight into their students' performance in the classroom, so they can have access to their strengths and weaknesses; in the meantime, they are prone to figure out closely and meticulously students' ways of thinking and the setbacks hindering them from reading or writing effeciently. In *A Dictionary of Literary Terms and Literary Theory*, Cuddon (2013) notes that reader-response criticism:

> [C]oncerned the relationship between text and reader and reader and text, with the emphasis on the different ways in which a reader participates in the course of reading a text and the different perspectives which arise in the relationship. Thus, reader-response theory is concerned with the reader's contribution to a text, and it challenges, with varying degrees of plausibility and conviction, the text-oriented theories of Formalism and New Criticism, which tend to ignore or underestimate the reader's role. (p. 559)

There is a consensus among academics that reader-response criticism emerged as a reaction against the New Criticism, or the Formalist Approach that dominated literary criticism for roughly a half-century. Unlike the preceding approach, which considers a piece of literature as an art object with an existence of its own not necessarily related to its potential readers, its author or the context in which it was produced (Guerin, 2005), reader-response criticism goes in an opposite direction assigning equal importance both to the reader and the context of text production and reception. It does not focus solely on the text per se in as much as it moves beyond it to explore other dimensions of meanings and values that the text eclipses for its potential audience.

Crouch and Rutherford (2014) posit that reader-response theory was influenced to a large extent by phenomenology, a philosophy based on individual perception and a manner of thinking that viewed human consciousness not merely as an inert registration of the world, but rather as actively constituting it. Phenomenology, which was inaugurated by German philosopher Edmund Husserl (1859-1938), contends that objects in the world – such as books– exist only when experienced by an active consciousness, or reader. Although the denomination was not in circulation with Greek philosophers, it is believed that Plato made use of it when he dismissed poets from his ideal state as he was alert to the profound effects of literature on people. (Herman et al., 2005) According to Davis and Womack (2002):

> Reader-response criticism devotes considerable attention to the act of reading itself, particularly in terms of the many different ways in which readers respond to literary texts ... As a theoretical paradigm, reader-response criticism explores three principal questions: do our various responses to literary works produce the same (or similar) readings?; can literary texts genuinely enjoy as many meanings as readers are able to create?; are some readings essentially more valid and justifiable than others? (p. 51)

It ought to go without saying that this school of thought conceives the text as a dead entity, non-existent, unless it is read and consumed by certain readers, who, by virtue of their prior knowledge and individual experiences, make it what it is. To elucidate, readers have a share in the construction of meaning in the text; they are able to recreate and reproduce it in a marvellous way according to their understanding abilities and cognitive competences. Accordingly, reader-response criticism proffers students numerous strategies for a better grasp and exploration of literary productions.

For literary historians, the critical heyday of this approach to literature started in the 1970s and experienced some turning points in the present era; the paradigm's foci, however, dates back to the twentieth century in the ancient Greek and Roman cultures that viewed literature as a rhetorical stratagem for influencing and manipulating people's reactions. Hence, with its roots in the text, reader-response criticism accounts for what is happening in the reader's mind during the process of reading a text. As Meyer (2003) notes:

> [A]ll reader-response critics aim to describe the reader's experience of a work: in effect we get a reading of the reader, who comes to the work with certain expectations and assumptions, which are either met or not met. Hence the consciousness of the reader – produced by reading the work – is the subject matter of reader-response critics. Just as writing is a creative act, reading is, since it also produces a text. (p. 1520)

A burgeoning interest in the reading activity appeared in the 1930s as a reaction against any attempts to downgrade or underestimate the reader's pivotal contribution to the construction or reproduction of meaning that was common with New Criticism -- a movement that prevailed in the 1940s and 1950s. This critical practice emphasized a close reading of poetry to fathom how a creative work of literature operated and functioned as an independent aesthetic object, the meaning of which can be attained without reliance on paralinguistic elements, such as the beliefs and attitudes of the author or the reader.

The New Critics believed that the timeless meaning of the text – what the text is – contained in the text alone. Its meaning is not a product of the author's intention and does not change with the reader's response. Reader-response theory, argues that what a text is cannot be disengaged from what it does. Therefore, the precursors of this theory share two assumptions: (1) that the role of the reader cannot be discarded from our understanding of literature and (2) that readers do not passively consume the meaning presented to them by an objective literary text; rather they actively make the meaning they find in literature. (Tyson, 2006) This implies that in the end, the major concern of reader-response theory is doubtlessly the readers and the obstacles that they encounter in the reading process. Without readers and reading, as McQuillan (1999) argues, "there would be no such thing as Literature. Books which are not read are merely ornaments on a shelf made from paper and ink."

Reader-response theory owes a lot to I.A. Richards, who led a series of classroom experiments with his undergraduate students at Cambridge University. During class, he would hand out sets of four poems, without indicating their various authors, and invite his students to comment upon them freely. His subsequent lecture would both explicate the poems and the discrepancies in his students' responses. Richards' intention was to unveil the diversity and the internal consistency of the interpretations. (qtd. in Kern, 2000)

Among the theorists that have probed into the functions and utilitarian tenets of reader- response theory is Rosenblatt (1994), who claimed that a text, once it leaves its author's hands, becomes hollow and senseless until an assumed reader resuscitates it. She saw the reader as transacting with a text to create what she called the poem, the meaning that emerges from the transaction at a given time. Feelings are evoked not just by the text, but by the text combining with the reader's present mood and purposes. The most significant idea in such a claim is that "the reader's creation of a poem out of a text must be an active, self-ordering and self-corrective process." (Rosenblatt, 1994, p. 11)

Schieble (2010) has challenged English teachers of literature to examine applications of reader-response theory in teaching reading, which claims that readers approach a text from two stances: 'aesthetic' (emotional) or 'efferent' (literal). He introduced a case study of pre- service English teachers and adolescents' web-based discussions about a work of young adult fiction. He pointed out that pre-service teachers' framing of questions caused the adolescents to deploy an aesthetic standpoint vis-à-vis the text. In their adoption of the aesthetic stance, readers are permitted to taste closely its simple and complex situations, and its characters and mull over the emotions as well as the images and events they come across.

Whiteley and Canning (2017) have examined the centrality of reader-response theory in contemporary Stylistics and focused on work that explicitly investigates such responses through the collection and analysis of extra-textual datasets. As they observed reader- response research in Stylistics is characterized by a commitment to rigorous and evidence- based approaches to the study of readers' interactions with and around texts, and the application of such datasets in the service of stylistic concerns: to contribute to stylistic textual analysis and/or wider discussion of stylistic techniques and methods. These researchers have lavished much attention to reading and the reader. They wanted to answer the very aching questions underpinning the problematic of textual sense and meaning: Which factors impact on readers' reactions to a certain text? What occurs when meaning is arcane or blurred?

7.3 Motivational Poetry

To whet students' appetite for reading and reacting to motivational poetry in a creative fashion, I opted for Walter D. Wintle's poem, "Thinking" – a poem that stresses a wide range of character traits that human beings ought to possess in order to realize their full potentials. Character traits including but not limited to self-confidence, trusting one's abilities, hopefulness, self-efficacy and intrinsic motivation are mandatory if people, students in particular, aspire to climb on the pyramid of self-actualization and triumph. When they are short of the already-mentioned character traits, they encounter various predicaments in their social and academic lives.

The poem demonstrates that mindsets exert an enormous impact on one's day-to-day conduct and performance. In other words, mindsets determine not only our victory and defeat in whatever life battle we engage in, but they also trigger our psychotherapy or melancholia. It is an inspirational poem *par excellence* as it encourages us, on the one hand, to persevere and spurs us to think big and be more ambitious in life adventures however daunting they might be. I, therefore, argue that any poem that lifts students' spirits higher or that supports them psychologically and emotionally on their academic voyage can be included under the umbrella term of motivational poetry. For Jones (2008, p. 14), a motivational poem designates "any poetic expression that insights the mind with revelation that encourages the heart to be stronger and inspires the will to do something that raises the spirit to another level."

Such poetry is meant to improve people's characters in their quotidian lives so that they can remain positive and never give up in difficult situations and circumstances. The objective of this poetry goes in tandem with Carroll (2005), who had used poetry to help people get access to the wisdom they already have but cannot experience because they cannot find the words in ordinary language. The reading and writing poetry activities are thus amenable to diminishing students' fears about end-term exams and curing their anxieties in life in general, with the intention of nurturing the best versions of themselves and leading them to show a great performance in life and at their universities and colleges in specific terms.

7.4 Guidelines and Signposts

Ninety-eight students have carefully read and responded to Walter D. Wintle's poem, "Thinking" following the teacher's guidelines and signposts for the weekly stylistic analysis, which usually takes the form of an essay comprising 3 to 5 paragraphs. Some questions were proposed as a starting point to enable the students to react to the poem creatively and enthusiastically. Among the questions addressed to them, we can cite the following ones: 1) Did the poem change your mood / disposition now? While reading the poem, 2) how were you feeling by then? 3) Which line touched your heart deeply? 4) How can you describe the style of the poem? As a reader, 5) what makes this poem unique and special for you? Eventually, 6) can you be more creative and add four lines (a quatrain) to enhance the core of the poem and complement its didactic tinge and tone? You can start with the same opening: "If you think ..."

7.5 Creativity and Selective Attention

The same text (the poem) was handed out to all the students to read individually and to react creatively to it. The word text means that the marks on the page – the words and the structures – appear the same for all the students.

The flexibility of the qualitative method I followed allows me as a teacher to swap roles between the students and myself since I also become a reader of their creative works, not only enjoying but also judging their originality, or say, their stylistic rigour and flavour. Hence, I depart from Rosenblatt's concept of "selective attention', which claims that readers invariably make choices, both conscious and subconscious. These choices, on which the concept of style itself is based, are more likely to have a space in their creative and poetic reactions. For instance, they may privilege specific grammatical constructions or favour certain lexical items over others because they are more evocative and expressive of their emotional and psychological states.

7.5.1 The Power of Simplicity

Considering the creative reactions students of Semester 6 at Ibn Zohr University, gave to Walter D. Wintle's poem, "Thinking", I may venture that they were all involved as active / creative readers; they felt they were the target audience of his motivational poem. They were consequently accorded a chance to bring their unswerving thoughts into a real-life context, and this has been eased by the simple repetitions of grammatical structures, mainly the if-clause and the accessible vocabulary and dictions of the poem. It is up to them to choose which way of thinking they must dwell on to feed their souls and minds with; that is, what their minds tell them is most likely to be true, and these mental suggestions work almost like magic, forcing them to make or not make the first move into their future goals and plans.

It is crystal clear that the poem has helped the students to boost their self-reflection and introspection as well as mirror their pre-occupations and life concerns through the stunning poetic words they have read and captured. As far as some students are concerned, the target audience of the poem could also be the poet himself, which implies that he wants to cheer himself up and stimulate his mind to pursue paths of optimism and positivism: the lines are akin to a positive self-talk that he embraces to counter the hardships and intermittent meltdowns hampering him from achieving success and veritable comfort. To fulfill such a purpose, he inserted some stylistic tropes such as sound patterning, indexicality with its variants (i.e., person deictics and time deictics), along with anaphora that make the poem melodious and euphonic. Indeed, these devices do not complexify the intent of the poem as it does not subsume hard to swallow expressions that need more simplifications and lucidity either from the teacher or the dictionary. Owing to the simplicity of the style, the poem received much appreciation from the students, who acknowledged that they have read it more than 10 times, for they wanted to grasp its message and artful imagery and, at the same time, enjoy the beauty of its vibrant style and cadence

7.5.2 Mindsets and Dispositions Matter

Students' penchant for and fondness of "Thinking" is also prominent in the way they have articulated their feelings and attitudes about it; they have initiated some positive and engaging reactions that attest to the great interest they have found in its theme and underlying message. They seem to agree that the poem, directly or obliquely, prompts them to think positively and to believe strongly in themselves. Besides, it inculcates good personality traits such as hope and optimism in their minds and psyche, urging them to undertake a psychological transformation and paving the ground for them to rethink their old habits and depressive moods. Undeniably, the reading of the poem transformed their mind frames and attitudes toward themselves and toward life in general. To produce their lines, the students have to enlarge their scope of attention to include, as Rosenblatt (2005) notes, the personal, affective aura as well as any associations surrounding the words evoked; they must not forget the experience, the moods and situations being created through the transaction.

Since the text appears to fall within the scope of their interests, they did not hesitate to recreate its denotative and connotative meanings according to their proper cultural experiences, imagination, cultural values and beliefs. While transacting with the poem, one student, for instance, has declared: "I was feeling happy, zestful and comfortable." Another student has written, "I felt motivated, more enlightened, bolder and proactive." A third student confessed that he was relieved, hopeful and reassured. Still, there is one student who admitted that she was in a cycle of being optimistic and pessimistic, happy and unhappy. This last reaction is unsurprising because the poem itself taps into these conflicting thoughts and contradictory emotions in human beings. Let us explore in Table 7.1 how some students have shown their prowess and sense of creativity while reacting individually to the written text of the poem:

Table 7.1: Students' creative reactions to "Thinking"

N.	Creative reactions	Positive dictions used	Metaphorical images
1.	If you think you are alone, you are not If you think someone can stop you, he can't If you think it's late, it's never late.	------------	If you think someone can stop you, he can't

2.	If you have a strong will You will surpass the storm You just need to be patient You just need to be strong Stay focused and reach your goal.	strong; will; patient; focused; goal	You will surpass the storm
3.	If you think you're able to do the impossible The world will come to help you If you see life in a lightening eye Your world will be charming.	think; able; help lightening; charming	You see life in a lightening eye Your world will be charming
4.	If you think you are not worthy, you are not If you think you are courageous, you are If you think, you can make it, you will We are just a mirror of what we think we are.	courageous	We are just a mirror of what we think we are
5.	If you think you will, sure you do As long as you flow, the dreams come true Don't hold back, whatever they say Don't turn back.	do; flow; dreams	You flow Don't hold back Don't turn back
6.	If you think you're lost, then you set yourself apart For where no fellow can reach your heart; But you, only with a pinch of art. If you think you're dead, think twice and outsmart.	fellow; art; outsmart	You set yourself apart Think twice and outsmart
7.	If you think you can do it, you'll do it It's your decision So make the good one You only get ONE LIFE!	do; decision; good; life	You only get ONE LIFE!

8.	If you think you are talented, you are If you think you are creative, you are If you think you are successful, you are Success starts out from your mind.	talented; creative; successful; success	Success starts out from your mind.
9.	If you think it's easy, so it is If you think you can't try, you'll never try If you think you'd get to the top, you won't stop Things go down and up, so don't give up.	try; top; up	Things go down and up, so don't give up
10.	If you think it's the end, just think again Fairness is a good reaction And courage is a decision.	fairness; courage	Courage is a decision
11.	If you think you deserve to thrive, then strive Be a tireless bearer of hope; Be a magnet, in this equation You've got to be humble; you've got to breathe hope.	thrive; strive; tireless; hope; a magnet; humble, breathe	Be a tireless bearer of hope You've got to breathe hope
12.	If you think you are down, you are Even if you grieved, you grew Even if you are hurt, you healed Even if you're tired, you tried.	grew; healed; tried	Even if you grieved, you grew

The rationale of the exercise on creative poetry, either through reading or writing, was geared towards empowering students and supporting them both emotionally and psychologically in their academic journey and university life. Sometimes, they might feel stressed, anxious and less excited about their studies, especially if they are overcome by laziness, homesickness or/and the overloaded university modules they should undertake in the final term before graduation. To help them bypass any sign of weakness and passivity, I have chosen "Thinking" because I staunchly believe that people's mindsets can determine their success or failure. There simply is no substitute for having positive thinking because it brings trust and hope. It gives one the motivation, energy and ability to succeed; it enables people to be happy and keep them going through the toughest times. (Hasson, 2017)

A first glance at the creative reactions in Table 7.1 showcases that the poem, aside from the fact that it moved the students emotionally and psychologically, it unleashes their imagination about the marvels of hope and positive self-talk. It is not coincidental that some of them kept the same grammatical structure of the If-clause as it communicates the trust and faith that they ought to put in themselves if they want to be successful and inspiring to others. This means that self-confidence can guarantee the appealing and desirable outcomes which students aspire to see in their lives. Of particular note here is that their creative reactions reveal much awareness about the style and aesthetics of the poem and the dominant theme or subsidiary themes of its text. The reactions, as Rosenblatt (1994) posits, start like the others, but quickly articulate the realization that this text is to be read and responded to as a poem.

In their transactions with the poem, students have gone further to create their own versions by initiating well-crafted expressions and significant metaphorical images that raise awareness about the potency of positive thinking and stimulating self-talk. Allusions to loneliness, discouragement by others, the tendency of some individuals to advance excuses because of time constraints, willingness and patience (self-directedness), the necessity of setting goals, self-determination, seeking support and guidance from others (other- directedness), self-worth and endurance, not to mention fairness, modesty and self-growth are the numerous lessons we can derive and extrapolate from students' creative reactions to "Thinking" at first sight. One reaction that I have myself read several times with much pleasure and enjoyment is Creative Reaction 11, wherein one student wrote the following uplifting and delightful words:

> If you think you deserve to thrive, then strive
> Be a tireless bearer of hope;
> Be a magnet, in this complex equation of life
> You've got to be humble and breathe hope.

What caught my attention in the previous lines is the pleasant tone and gratifying metaphors that the student deployed to express the idea of hope and optimism. Regardless of what happens, one has to breathe hope and be a bearer of hope – working tremendously hard as a source of inspiration for oneself and for others around. This responsive reading is deemed more valid than the others not because it is systematic but because it is full of sophistication and artistry at the level of style and the poetic expression. The student poet has embellished her lines with emotive and cognitive elements and she was able to touch her peers' hearts readily and effortlessly. Thus, I can say that the poem turns so meaningful when the students interact cleverly with its metaphors and diction to germinate their personal meanings and self-reflections.

The creative reading of the poem is something in which the students have a role and something that takes place over a particular period of time. It is, according to Wolfreys (1999), only when they actually read (actively participate in the building of meaning) that the poem might be said to exist. When we consider Creative Reaction 1, 2 and 3, we realize that the student poets viewed "Thinking" from the viewpoint of determination and willingness. Seemingly, they encouraged their counterparts to stay patient and to look optimistically to fulfill their aspirations and to be oblivious to storms and negative people. This is recurrent in Creative Response 5, where one student asked his fellows not to give up or look back despite mockery and austere criticism. This attitude has been portrayed by another student as self- worth (i.e., self-esteem), which requires one to demonstrate aptness and courage when facing dilemmas and hazardous experiences in life. If we read students' responses and creative reactions as one whole, we realize that they somehow grasped the words and their associations on account of the emotional imprint it left on their psyche. Rosenblatt (1994) writes:

> Apprehension of what a poem is "about," what a novel "says," the human meaning, the "sense" of the words, what they refer to "in the world" is an essential element, which cannot be dissociated from the affective impact on the reader, given an aesthetic orientation. (p. 42)

Regarding Creative Reaction 6 and 7, the student poets juxtaposed negative thinking with defeat, loss and even death. They do not deviate from espousing self-efficacy and aptness since they are an art that sets people into motion and vigour. Astonishingly, the student in Creative Response 7 has tapped on graphology to stress the idea that human beings have only one life, and they are to decide on what is more appropriate to them. In what concerns Creative Reaction 8, 9 and 10, the student poets have equated success with thinking, struggle and perseverance, fairness and courage. What is at stake is that everything springs from the mind, which seems to control not only people's actions but their destiny as well.

Creative Reaction 12 is also beset with a sense of creativity and shrewdness, for the student poet played with sounds to entertain the reader and retain the contradictions embedded in Wintle's poem. What this student says is that pain and grief might function like forces that build people's personae and characters. He seems to suggest that an individual is capable of the process of healing and self-recovery irrespective of past wounds and bygone afflictions. His sense of creativity is salient not only in the conflicting ideas he fronted intentionally but also in the rhetorical exploitation of alliteration (g / h / t) and anagrams (tired / tried), each of which betrays an affinity for motivational poetry and a craving after self- growth and development.

> If you think you are down, you are
> Even if you grieved, you grew
> Even if you are hurt, you healed
> Even if you're tired, you tried.

The creative reactions to "Thinking" as advanced by the students tell much about the genres of texts they want to see and study in the classroom; likewise, they pinpoint their roles as active agents who impart novel dimensions of meaning, creativity and another identity to the text in question. Because their interpretations varied, their creative reactions were neither consistent nor homogeneous as shown above in Table 7.1. Accordingly, all the students conceived of the poem as a masterpiece and a work of art, allowing them to express their thoughts and feelings more freely and eloquently. Their creative readings were unobtrusively interactive and dynamic, which accounts for the variety of their reactions and spellbinding metaphorical images they have employed and wonderfully crafted. As Karolides (2000) points out:

> Because of this, the relationship between reader and text is dynamic. The reader responding is also dynamic, alive to stimulus and response. Further, what a reader makes of a text will reflect the reader's state of being at a particular time and place and in a particular situation, as well as the reader's relationship to the text. (p. 6)

The dynamic response to the poem is also manifest in the pronouns they have all exploited to vehicle the blessings of positive thinking and a bright outlook. Pronouns such as "you" (n=61); "it" (n=8), "We" (n=3) direct the readers and shape their expectations and actions. As soon as they have read their end products, I felt they were not only addressing their peers but also motivating themselves through positive self-talk, as expressed or recommended by Walter D. Wintle. They told themselves they could do anything and make it happen since their brains had learned how to think defiantly and function more appropriately. Consider Table 7.2, which illustrates the main pronouns students have used in their creative reactions to "Thinking":

Table 7.2: Frequency of pronouns used in the sample

Pronoun	Frequency	Functions
You	61	Subject
It	8	Subject & object
We	3	Subject
Your	3	Possessive adjective
Yourself	1	Reflexive
He	1	Subject
They	1	Subject
Someone	1	Indefinite

As can be seen, the subject pronoun "you" stands centre stage as opposed to other pronouns, be they reflexive, object or even indefinite. The usage of the deictic expression "you", in the 12 sampled creative reactions, engages the writer and the reader to be alert to negative ways of thinking because they make people feel bad and incapable. Presumably, it appears that students' creative reactions are identical to the model studied, yet a second examination of their written pieces proves that students have set the poem in motion, and so set themselves in motion too. (Iser, 1980) As a result, their creative reactions encapsulate the positive terms they have integrated imaginatively, the compelling metaphorical images and expressions they have penned and the hopeful dispositions they willy-nilly fostered in the reader.

7.6 Advantages of Reader-Response Theory

Undoubtedly, reader-response theory is a useful tool for probing into students' reading and writing skills, each of which is influenced by their prior knowledge. Sometimes, the reading activity can be daunting if the text to be studied and commented upon involves abstract topics and complex grammatical and lexical structures; however, when the students are encouraged to use their sense of creativity, they can take risks in terms of reading and responding to texts. Hence, reader-response theory may be, as Adams, (1931) observes,

> [W]ell suited to L2 writing instruction involving reading and writing, because students themselves may not see a connection between the acts of reading and writing and might perform one act in isolation from the other, even when they are reading a source text for a writing assignment. (p. 53)

Unlike the Stylistics' class, students are instructed in both reading and writing separately. In the module of Writing Paragraphs or Composition, they are given topics to write about or general statements to react to; they are taught to use academic English, create cohesion and respect grammatical rules and mechanics such as capitalization and punctuation. In the Reading Comprehension course, considerable attention is allocated to the promotion of the reading skill, which alternates between drawing inferences and paraphrasing, and occasionally between knowing the meaning of certain vocabulary items and identifying the central idea. Nevertheless, when they are invited to summarize texts in their own words, students can switch from one skill to another. In fact, it is this horizontal link bonding reading and writing together that the Stylistics course aims to establish.

It is assumed that reader-response theory enables the teacher to involve all the students in the learning process since there is no right or wrong answer. What matters first and foremost to him is that they react to the text in their proper ways by using appropriate language and good analytical skills, a fact which lessens their panic and anxiety while thinking freely and creatively. In this way, the reader-oriented approach "empowers them by showing them that they, not the text (or not the text alone), are at the center of reading. It tells them that they have a legitimate, meaning-making role to play while reading." (Hirvela, 2004, p. 53)

But what does it mean to write a creative reaction to Walter D. Wintle's poem, "Thinking"? For some students, it meant the use of positive dictions and expressive metaphorical images that appeal to the teacher and the students alike. To others, it signified the soundness of imagination and the overflow of their feelings and convictions – what they might be lacking in their personalities or what they want to see as emergent character traits nurturing their daily behaviours and entire being.

Given that "Thinking" revolves around life and hopefulness, positivity and self-confidence, the students did not proceed with writing their responses without embellishing the four lines with some catchy metaphors to ease understanding for the listener and reader. Such metaphors cannot be dissociated from meaning-making occurring inside and outside of the classroom. As Wormeli (2009) puts it,

> Because metaphors and analogies are really about meaning-making, and meaning-making is the primary goal for classroom instruction, we can easily see the importance of: (1) being aware of students' backgrounds as we choose and use metaphors and analogies, and (2) creating the background knowledge that will enable students to use the intended metaphor for deeper meaning. (p. 41)

One of the assets of the reader-response approach to poetry I have accommodated in the Stylistics' course is that it enthuses students to read poetry in a creative and responsive way. This pedagogical approach does not impose on them a rigid or stringent model of analysis, which can live up to the expectations of some students and frustrate several others. Instead, it is a malleable approach that urges them to think like "poets talking to themselves." (qtd. in Rosenblatt's, 1994, p. 2) The guidelines initiated before the creative reading and writing processes are, in fact, nothing but a toolkit to propel them to relish and appreciate the art of poetry, and why not experiment with its complex style in order that they can produce their own pieces as much skillfully as they can.

7.7 Conclusion

This chapter has delved into the evolution of reader-response theory and its numerous assets in the Stylistics classroom; it expounded on the mutual interaction between the text and the reader, who reportedly assumes an active role as he/she engages in the processes of reading and interpretation – two stages that increase his/her intellectual and emotional involvement. Such theory brings students to the hub of learning because they can express themselves freely and talk about their individual experiences more creatively. Once their creative reactions start to be the focus of the teacher's attention, the students feel more intrigued by the text they read and display an unprecedented affinity for learning. Without their responses, the text does not have any existence and identity, and it remains just ink splashed on paper. In the next chapter, I endeavour to study the style and complex meanings of home, as well as positive thinking in pandemic poetry, and I focus mainly on Ketty O'Meara's virtual poem, "And the People Stayed Home."

7.8 Further Readings

Chew, C. R., DeFabio, R., & Honsbury, P. (1986). *Reader response in the classroom*. New York: New York State English Council.

Clifford, J. (1991). *The experiences of reading: Louise Rosenblatt and reader-response theory*. Michigan: Boynton/Cook Publishers.

Many, J., & Cox, C. (1992). *Reader stance and literary understanding: Exploring the theories, research and practice*. New York: Ablex Publishing Corporation.

Price, M. (1989). *Reader-response criticism: A test of its usefulness in a first year college course in writing about literature*. New York: Peter Lang.

Shelton, K. Y. (1994). *Reader response theory in the high school English classroom*. Winston-Salem: NC: Wake Forest University.

7.9 Questions for Discussion

1) What is reader-response theory?
2) Is reception theory the same as reader-response theory?
3) How can you describe motivational poetry?
4) In your view, when can students show their creativity in the reading and analysis of poetry?
5) Why should teachers use the reader-response approach in L2?
6) Are there any shortcomings of this method of learning?

Chapter 8

THE PANDEMIC HOME IN PANDEMIC POETRY: "AND THE PEOPLE STAYED HOME"

Highlights:

- *Home is considered as an interior space that provides warmth and cordiality*
- *Poets have been enthralled by the notion of home.*
- *O'Meara's pandemic home can satisfy people's lower and higher needs.*
- *Human beings have experienced healing and convalescence in the home of the pandemic.*
- *The style of pandemic poetry is different from the traditional one.*

8.1 Introduction

This chapter, which departs from the theory of "hierarchy needs" and the notion of "mind style", describes the register of the pandemic "home" and see poets' perceptions of it during the recent global lockdown. Mind style alludes to any linguistic presentation of an individual mental self; it suggests the ways of looking at reality no matter how painful it is. The term also indicates, not the object referred to in a text, but the way in which that object is seen, the way in which – the world is apprehended, or conceptualized. One question is begged in this critical enquiry to better the social and academic life of students: How did poets of the global lockdown view the pandemic home in their pandemic poetry? First, let us examine some views that poets allocated to the ordinary home.

8.2 Binding People Together

Poets have excelled in the rendering of "home" in their poetic productions and creative works. They crafted imaginary spaces of cohabitation and warmth, providing shelter and the necessary psychological backup to vulnerable people – those suffering from trauma, panic and excessive anxiety. The Irish poet, George Augustus Moore (1852- 1933), once wrote that a person can travel around the world in search of what he/she needs, and they return to their homes to find it. Returning to homes implies that "home" per se is not a physical setting, nor is it a building comprising a door, walls and windows; in fact, the concept of "home" transcends any antiquated view about geography, locality or even housing. Hence, "home" functions like a haven for people, their families and friends. Robert Frost (1874-1963) posits that homes are the venues where -- when a person has to go there, the inhabitants will be more excited to take him/her in.

Despite its heterogeneous meanings, "home" remains an essential human right and an ingredient of a dignified life. (Holdsworth & Morgan, 2005) It is the place of old reminiscence, the location of childhood memories, the melting pot of love stories. As a mythical space, it bears psycho-emotional references, bestowing upon people the ability to speak to others freely and live by their sides harmoniously. That is, it binds people together and fortifies their social interactions, nurturing and renurturing senses of coziness and comfort amongst them. With the upsurge of COVID-19 pandemic and the global lockdown, people started to look at their homes from a different lens. While the public space was almost deserted, the private sphere was a haven for parents and their children. The family was the hub of all social relationships because the pandemic reinvigorated human connections between its members. Through the poetry that flourished in the age of coronavirus – COVID-19 pandemic, poets have initiated a wide range of definitions and conceptions of "home." They recorded the masses' responses to the pathogen and vehicled their preoccupations and interactions at the private and domestic spheres.

What is more, poets pictured "home" as a versatile and multi-faceted setting, sheltering parents and their families, catering to their day-to-day needs and basic wants. The "home" of the lockdown poetry is obviously a special home that provides both emotional security and intimacy, love and physical well-being, balance and positivity. It is a home that de- traumatizes its inhabitants -- ridding them of loneliness and anxiety, depression and even panic. This home has by no means strengthened familial ties and connected friends to cope with the new challenges of living and surmount the draconian measures set on travel and movement. It is a home that provides almost everything. (Risi et al., 2021)

Food, worship, gaming, and other social practices were all included in the homes of the global pandemic. This is confirmed by Aridi (2021), who argues that "home has shifted from being a launchpad to being a whole space station. It has become our world on earth: theater, school, restaurant, office, gym." The elderly found in it serenity and tranquillity; the young saw in it a place of opportunity and even creativity. Homes themselves are true resources for setting up friendships, love and building social relationships. (Rix et al., 2005) These novel meanings of "home" can be ascribed to the closure of the exterior space and the opening of the interior space that is apt to immunize people against the virus. The infected cases have been spreading like wildfire, with many deaths ever recorded in human history.

Across the globe, the overwhelming majority of people have been reported as feeling uncomfortable and even frustrated. They displayed a wide range of symptoms, such as insomnia, schizophrenia, and emotional distress. However, the new atmosphere of the "home" helped diminish the human fear of the unknown. Nobody knew what life would look like after the lockdown, yet the only thing that people deeply fathomed is that "home" was the sole place they would stay in or go to in order to triumph over pain and regain their balance and convalescence. Such home, as Scott (2008) points out, enabled people to be themselves. It paved the ground for them to do what they cannot do in the real world.

8.3 Prior Research on Home

Annison (2000) delved into the arcane meaning of "home" and endeavoured to restore the term's descriptive value by identifying its meaning through reference to the intellectual disability and mainstream professional literature. He concluded that "home" is a multi-faceted concept with no single contributing attribute. Following the same frame of mind, Easthope (2010) explored the notion of "home" in connection with place and housing. The home, as she argues, is a doubtlessly significant type of place that provides insights into the relationship between places and people's identities as well as their psychological well-being; the dynamics of conflicts surrounding home-places; and the political economy of home places.

Gillsjö and Schwartz-Barcott (2011) have, in turn, examined the concept of "home" and its meaning in the lives of three older adults. The results yielded that the adults spoke of childhood, community, residential, church and heavenly homes. Feelings of comfort and security were associated with residential homes, peace and quiet with church homes, safety and pleasure with heavenly homes. Whether appertaining to the lockdown or to the pandemic, "home' helped people relax, meditate and dangle. That is, it is the place where they are protected and warmly welcomed. This goes in tandem with Doiron's (2013) view that "home" is the site where human beings understand each other, love one another unconditionally, no matter how badly one screws up.

The common trait between all these standpoints is that they portrayed "home" as a sanctuary that safeguards people against all potential risks and hazards. As a result, "home" proffers people numerous choices: they can choose what to eat and when, who to invite in and who to exclude, what clothes to wear, and when to go to bed. According to Pughe and Philpot (2007):

> A home is more than a house, more than four walls. How we decorate and look after where we live, what is hung on the walls, the care with which furniture is brought and cared for, how ornaments and momentos of holidays are displayed – all these things are what turn a house into a home. A home will say much about who lives in it and how they regard it and themselves. (p. 53)

The most popular maxims: "home sweet home"; "there is no place like home"; "home is where the heart is"; "home is a shelter from storms – all sorts of storms", arguably, point to the great significance of "home" in the lives of individuals and their communities -- the relief and pleasure they encounter when they return to it. At the very core of the issue is the assumption that before a home becomes home, or even before human relationships evolve into home, it is mandatory that warmth, belonging, esteem, and emotional care forge this particular environment. In this regard, Reynolds (2013) maintains that a "home" is something deeper within us that comes out of us to become a home.

In this chapter, "home" means not only the place people inhabit but it also signifies a sense of feeling secure and being at ease with oneself and others. It is inclusive of the diverse activities which people took up during the global lockdown. The exponential curve of the pandemic worldwide forced people to stay home and observe specific measures to avoid infections. The family regained its role as its members congregated to ensure its unity and continuity. By the same token, "home" becomes a place of healing from public fear, paranoia and collective trauma. It turned into a health institution that hosts inpatients because public hospitals were extremely full and overcrowded. Such a home accorded people a sense of belonging, and it immunized them against the pandemic.

8.4 And The People Stayed Home

One narrative prose poem is approached critically and stylistically to dismantle poets' perceptions of the concept of "home" during the pandemic. The prose poem, which is entitled: "And the People Stayed Home", was written by Kitty O'Meara on March 13, 2020. Over the past two years, it went viral on social media, and it has been translated into more than 20 languages. Likewise, it has been chanted and recited by several people as a song and a prayer in different social occasions. While some teachers have taught it to their students, other musicians have performed it live for their fans and followers. In so far as Krug (2020) is concerned, the poem

> [A]lso appears in "Together in a Sudden Strangeness: America's Poets Respond to the Pandemic," an anthology curated by Alice Quinn, former New Yorker poetry editor and former executive editor of the Poetry Society of America, alongside works by Ada Limón, Julia Alvarez, Billy Collins and other luminaries. (*The Washington Post*. Dec. 10, 2010)

The poetic response O'Meara gave to the pandemic demonstrates that poets tend to transcribe the masses' sufferings and afflictions with positive mind frame and compassion. Poets are not detached from people's ordeals and agonies because they own the stamina to render them visible to the public in an exciting and entertaining manner. Through the prism of language and metaphoricity, poets can promote a culture of dialogue and contribute to human connectivity, prompting people to discard negative sensations and melancholy from their thinking and feeling habits. When they visualize "home", they architect alternative places to dispose their fellow human beings of grief and sorrow. By doing so, they turn into engineers and architects, who are keen on manipulating the imaginary space and appropriating it to suit the pressing demands of the status quo. It is crystal clear that poets have shared the same concern for humanity as they responded to the pandemic in divergent ways to comfort people and appease their panicked and agitated selves.

8.5 A Mixed Stylistic Approach

Along with Maslow's (1943) pyramid of "hierarchy needs", Fowler's (1977) "mind style" is taken into account as it explicates the poet's text and talk, their worldviews and their determination to assist people to surpass the burdens and hurdles of the pandemic. Register as a configuration of meanings that are typically associated with a particular situational configuration of field, mode and tenor (Halliday & Hasan, 1985/1989) is also central to this analysis. Very often, these situations are associated with human activities and interests such as reading, meditating and bird-watching. As for "mind style", it points to the linguistic representation of a character's mental perception of the world. Fowler (1977) states that

> A mind style may analyze a character's mental life more or less radically may be concerned with the relatively superficial or relatively fundamental aspects of the mind; may seek to dramatize the order and structure of conscious thoughts, or just present the topics on which a character reflects, or display preoccupations, prejudices, perspectives

and values which strongly bias a character's worldview but of which s/he may be unaware. (p. 103)

The prose poem is analyzed qualitatively at the level of register and mind style. The linguistic choices made by the poet not only determine her worldview and mental description of home in the lockdown, but they also mirror her apprehensions of apropos self-quarantine and the wherefores of the pandemic on humanity. Now let us see how the prose poem addresses human lower and higher needs.

8.6 Meeting People's Needs

O'Meara was resolute in instilling hopefulness and optimism into people's thinking over the pandemic; she exposes them to the wider experience of their counterparts across the globe so that they can overcome claustrophobia – the fear of being in confined and enclosed spaces. (Clark & Pointon, 2016) Her narrative poem comprises 14 lines, each of which pictures an episode from the new system of living that confined children and their parents amidst walls and room structures. The most intriguing feature of the prose poem is its focalization on the idea of "home", which occupies a central position in the psyche of the speaker. The latter has transferred the outside world into the inside owing to the tough procedures undertaken to curb the virus. O'Meara has screened down the "home" of the pandemic as an interior world where people can practice all their recreations and leisure activities freely and safely. Homes, therefore, were not only shelters against COVID-19, but they were also sites for exercising, meditation, creativity and cultivation. Their multi-functional roles endowed people with the capacity to tolerate self-isolation and withstand the social distancing measures.

This milestone event compelled people to reshuffle space to satisfy their needs. Following Maslow's (1943) pyramid of hierarchy needs, it can be argued that homes allowed people to meet lower and deficiency needs such as sleep, rest, food and drink. Likewise, they catered to their safety, belonging and esteem needs. As opposed to the exterior space, the interior space was deemed more secure and safer for people to stay in because of the contagion. Most importantly, the pandemic home can be regarded as an arena of competitiveness, innovation and academic excellence. Students, for instance, have made great achievements and received several awards and prizes from their schools and institutions thanks to their successful performances. Professors, on the other hand, took part in a wide range of conferences and symposia through video and audio conferencing, for which they got both appreciation and recognition. Accordingly, the pandemic home helped people attain their short and long-term goals; it allowed children to communicate esteem for their parents; it brought the members of the family together; meanwhile, it sheltered children and accorded them enough strength to move ahead towards success and self-fulfilment.

There are five levels of human needs, which are inborn and inherent in almost all human beings. These needs are ranked in terms of importance and hierarchy. Deficiency (also called lower needs) are very essential and ought to be satisfied before the growth and higher needs appear; so they might influence people's behaviour and manners. The most basic needs (physiological) are at the bottom of the pyramid, and they include hunger, thirst, rest and so on. They are followed by security and safety needs, which include shelter, stability, such as having a job and a monthly income, etc. Then, love and belonging need to involve friendship, intimacy and social proximity. Next, self-esteem needs to revolve around respect and the struggle for prestige and reputation. Eventually, at the top of the pyramid there exist self-actualization or self-fulfilment needs that include creativity and the achievements of one's goals. Consider Maslow's (1943) pyramid of hierarchy needs in Figure 8.1:

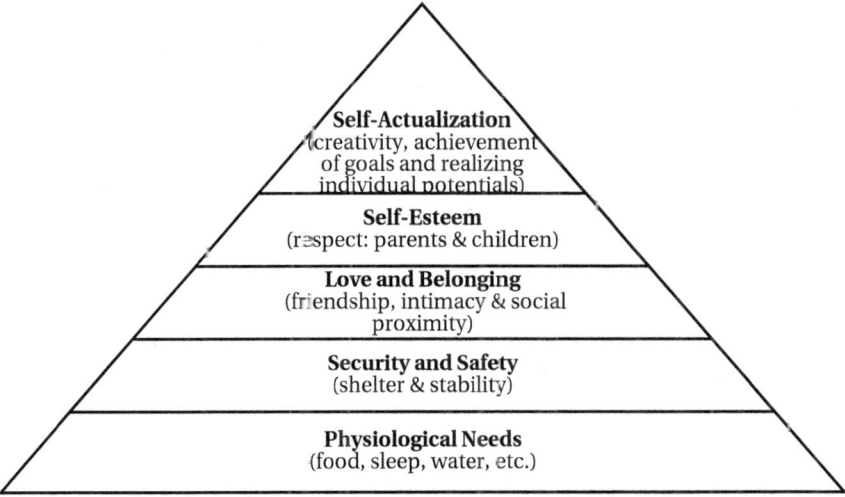

Figure 8.1: Maslow's (1943) pyramid of hierarchy needs

Undeniably, the physiological needs such as food, water and sleep are considered the most prepotent of all needs owing to the apparition of unusual modes of behavior such as panic buying. Once these lower needs are well gratified, the safety needs (security; stability; dependency; protection; freedom from fear, freedom from anxiety and chaos; order, law; and so on) are taken into account by the family in the home sphere. In fact, the safety needs have become urgent, especially with the increasing number of deaths and infections. This tends to be true for all human beings, including the healthy ones, since they were required to respond appropriately to the spread of the pandemic.

Besides the physiological and the safety needs, the love and affection as well as belongingness needs are fairly well gratified. The absence of friends was substituted for the presence of children and parents, all of whom exchanged affectionate relationships and mutual care to vanquish the global pathogen. Furthermore, the esteem needs were observed because the family system turned strong, stable and grounded on mutual respect. In some cases, certain people craved after uniqueness with all its ramifications -- glory, status, prestige, attention, dignity, appreciation, and the like. These higher needs boosted people's self-confidence, worth, capability, and adequacy of being useful and necessary in the world. Regarding the need for self-actualization, it could be spotted in their resolution to be themselves -- and thus remain true to their own nature. (Maslow, 1943) Although individual differences do exist at such level, they did not hamper the members of the family from giving the best versions of themselves: as parents desired to be ideal parents, their children struggled to maximize their distance learning to live up to their expectations.

When we consider the title of the poem, "And The People Stayed Home", we realize that the speaker is feeling absorbed in the pros of the pandemic than insinuating its cons. The usage of the coordinating conjunction "and" (n=20), besides establishing parallelism between the sequenced events, shows that the speaker attempts to liaise two facts: the first is totally backgrounded as it concerns the fierceness of the virus and its creeping nature, and the second is foregrounded on the grounds of the radical changes the virus caused in terms of movement and everyday activities. The harmony, which is begged in the poem through cohesion and alliteration (e.g., read / rested; meditated / met) and internal rhyme (e.g., games / ways), epitomizes the successful interactions people have built at the level of the family unit and interior space.

A quick survey of the poem's lexemes unveil that they relate to the lexical field of "home." Take, for example, mental and physical processes such as "stayed"; "read"; "listened"; "rested"; played"; "meditated"; prayed", "danced"; "think." These verbs become realizable only in the "home" sphere, for the outside sphere witnessed a dysfunction all of a sudden. Considering Fowler (1977), it can be said that the narrator (speaker) is examining people's mental selves and reporting the events from their proper perspectives to manufacture consensus about them. She invests on person deictics with the view to grab their full attention and rouse interest in the story told. Apparently, she distances herself from the events to neutralize the entire description so that it can appeal to a large audience. From people's viewpoint, the interior space, the physical home and the family in particular, can be considered as avenues for comfort and self-introspection. The apparition of the term "people" (n=5) along the lines of the poem clearly suggests that the speaker was engaged in the rendering of life events and the interpretation of the same events from the lens of specific individuals.

Thus, the narrative space that the poet sculpted makes the story engaging and appealing. The people concerned are not identified by any race, name or gender. They are represented as one homogeneous group that cherishes the same interests, hobbies and inclinations. Though the context is eclipsed, the poet gives ample clues and allusions across the lines to underscore the activities that people took up in their homes. Knowingly or unknowingly, she is pointing to every single activity that becomes meaningful in the pandemic home. This narrative practice has the potential to alter people's worldviews and guide them to what Afuape (2011) has called "preferred directions." That is, the poem directs the reader to concentrate on specific phenomena and forget others that do not fall into the poet's areas of interest.

8.7 Register and Contextual Parameters

Considering Halliday and Hasan's (1985/1989) contextual parameters, known as register, the field of the poem is home and human activities, its tenor are the narrator / speaker with her virtual readers, while the mode is written language that sounds like a prose poem. Figure 8.2 illustrates the register and contextual parameters of the poem:

Contextual Parameters	And the People Stayed Home
Field	Subject matter (home and human activities)
Tenor	Participants (the narrator / speaker and virtual readers)
Mode	Medium (simple, written prose poem)

Figure 8.2: The register and contextual parameters (see Flowerdew, 2013)

By situating the readers / listeners in their homes, the speaker resolves to close all other spaces in an attempt to unpack the conundrum of homes in the global lockdown. These homes were viewed as substitutes for other places. Almost any leisure activity seems to be feasible and doable inside them since homes themselves moved from rigidity to resilience and springiness. Children, for instance, can play their favourite games and learn new life skills; adults can meditate and perform their religious rituals as usual. However, the most remarkable effect of the pandemic is that human beings were able to meet their shadows. This image as opted for by the speaker indicates that humanity before the pandemic was somewhat disconnected, but it underwent a total metamorphosis in the global lockdown: parents would sit again with their children and watch over them. Equally important, children were able to intermingle with their parents and have fun with them. The other interpretation that seems worth-mentioning is that people had the chance to meet and explore themselves. Whatever reading we can give, the truth is that the pandemic brought humanity together, and it cemented interpersonal communication in the family system.

People have then found inspiring ways to overcome chaos and agitation. Though they were physically disengaged, they constructed virtual bridges of understanding, amity and dialogue between themselves. They promoted a communal spirit to combat the ferocity of the virus, and they showed that collectivity is a wise decision because it leads to and brings about empathy and solidarity. Irrespective of the social distance and self-quarantine, people seized the opportunity to sing, dance and play music to each other from their balconies and respective homes. This is probably what the speaker was alluding to when she said that some meditated, some prayed, and some danced.

8.8 Poetry, Faith and Healing

The marvellous value of the prose poetry read during the pandemic lies in its therapeutic and healing power. Such poetry thrived in the interior space and not outside of it, and, in the meantime, it contributed to people's mental well-being and self-recovery. No doubt, when people stay home, the earth takes a break, and the environment becomes clean and calm. The assets of the pandemic are seen not only in people's new mindsets and deportment but also in the regeneration and healing of Mother Nature. According to the poet, it is people's ignorance and carelessness that damages the earth and exacerbates air pollution.

Healing is emphasized in the poem due to the large number of infections, losses and deaths that took place with the increase of the pandemic. But what does healing truly mean? It means convalescence and recovery – to stop suffering and resume the daily routines with a new spirit and resolution. This is in utter agreement with Seamonds (1985), who maintains that healing "means being delivered from the prison of past hurts." Medical experts and therapists all agree that healing also signifies restoring to health and soundness; it is setting right, repairing and bringing forth recovery. (MacKey, 2009)

By considering "new choices" and "new images", as well as detailing on "new ways to live", the speaker unravels the countless lessons humankind took from the expansion of the pandemic. Among these lessons, one can cite the invaluable significance of societal bonds, the importance of spending time with family and loved ones, the need for a good health system, and the risks threatening planet Earth. The virus has also made people alert to life priorities and the incessant value of time, which seems to be overlooked by so many. It showcases that all human beings really need each other to survive and they are entailed to set aside differences for the public good.

There is no denying that the worldview, or say positive thinking, promoted in the poem is more likely to reinforce the readers' worldviews regarding their pandemic homes and the experiences they had of the recent global lockdown. Worldviews indicate beliefs and assumptions about the real world that impact on people's thoughts and behaviour. They are the views people hold about the big questions of life. (McFarland, 2014) The big questions of life revolve around truth, God, the origin of mankind, its destiny, the afterlife and so on. The poem is arguably not only a reflection on these views and questions but also an endorsement of faith because it chronicles the peace of mind that people encountered in their pandemic homes. It illustrates those good feelings, which they experience in their hearts and minds without being annoyed by the macabre situation of the outside world. Like the moving power of love and poetry, faith helps people feel more supported and peaceful with themselves and with others around them. In the words of Paz (2011)

> Faith is a seed that lies deep within us. When watered and nurtured, this seed will grow into a huge tree that will bear much fruit in our lives and in the lives of others. Once firmly rooted, faith is the foundation that keeps us grounded during the hurricanes of life. (p. ix)

This is applicable to life in the time of COVID-19 pandemic. The overwhelming majority of Americans, for instance, have claimed that their faith has deepened because of the coronavirus. (Boorstein, 2020) Although it is to some extent invisible and immeasurable, faith seems to predominate O'Meara's poetic scrutiny of and self-introspection about the pandemic home. Suffice it to say that the by-product of faith is recollection and stillness and these two mental and esoteric states can be easily induced from O'Meara's prose poem.

The problematizaton of "home" in poetry is not a nascent practice. Edgar Guest (1881- 1959) has written about home and its haunting memories, using spelling and grammar mistakes to impart a profound wisdom and common ground knowledge. Decades ago, Philip Larkin (1922-1985), too, composed a short poem entitled "Home is So Sad." The immense importance, which "home" gained in the poets' creative works, is symptomatic of the fact that "home" can be a person, an idea, a memory, a place or a feeling and that it is much more complex than we think. However, the most impressive line on "home" comes from the British-Canadian poet Robert William Service (1874-1958), who openly declared that angels' words in the Heaven are so sweet because they talk only of home and love.

8.9 Conclusion

This chapter, which is anchored in the theory of "hierarchy needs" and "mind style" has delved into the conception of home in pandemic prose poetry that thrived in the era of the global lockdown. O'Meara's soulful depiction of the new system of life during COVID-19 pandemic is truly an invitation for people to stay home to be safe and discover the splendour of the family and the private space. She introduced another meaning of "home" that encapsulates fun and meditation, pain and recovery, as well as recreation and jubilation. Whether of the pandemic or not, home remains problematic and unstable not because of social and external norms but because poets always add a new layer to it. The next chapter revisits the educational space, notably lecture-based instruction and learning styles, in a medieval university classroom.

8.10 Further Readings

Acim, R. (2021). Lockdown poetry, healing and the COVID-19 pandemic, *Journal of poetry therapy*, 34 (2), pp. 67-76, DOI:10.1080/08893675.2021.1899629

Clift, E. (Ed.). (2021). *A twenty first century plague: poetry from a pandemic.* Colorado Springs, CO: U Professors Press.

Dera, J. (2021). Evaluating poetry on COVID-19: Attitudes of poetry readers toward corona poems, *Journal of poetry therapy*, 34 (2), pp. 77-94, DOI:10.1080/08893675.2021.1899630

Guglielmo, A. (2022). [Review of the book *And the people stayed home*, by Kitty O'Meara]. *American book review*, 43 (1), pp. 25-28, DOI:10.1353/abr.2022.0004

Russo, M. T., Argandona, A., & Peatfield, R. (Eds.). (2022). *Happiness and domestic life: The influence of the home on subjective and social well-being.* London: Routledge.

8.11 Questions for Discussion

1) What are the major activities that people engaged in the pandemic home during the last global lockdown?

2) In your opinion, why did the pandemic home strengthen human ties / relationships in the family system?

3) Are there any other poets that have problematized "home" in poetry?

4) How can you define the concept of "mind style"?

5) Do you agree that the pandemic home has satisfied human lower and higher needs? Explain.
6) Who is the target audience of the poem? Give three arguments to back up your claim.

Chapter 9

LECTURING AND LEARNING STYLES: A MEDIEVAL CLASSROOM

> **Highlights:**
> - *There is a close connection between pedagogy and art.*
> - *The contemporary university classroom, be it physical or digital, hybrid or non-hybrid, has been inspired by the medieval university classroom.*
> - *The teacher's teaching style should match students' learning styles.*
> - *Artists can assist teachers to improve their teaching methodologies; so they can suit all types of learners.*
> - *Interactive lecturing is becoming a good alternative to traditional lecturing since it can guarantee interest and increase students' motivation for learning.*

9.1 Introduction

This chapter, which could be quite useful to students engaged in the study of Applied Linguistics and ELT, examines a painting by Laurentius de Voltolina, who capitalized on the power of art to portray the medieval classroom at the University of Bologna in Italy. To this end, Multimodal Discourse Analysis (MDA) is accommodated to systematically analyze the significance of the drawing to the twenty-first-century lectured-based university classroom. With this instrument in mind, I seek to respond to these questions:

Q1. What characteristics did teachers and students of the medieval age cherish either in the production or the reception of knowledge?
Q2. Is there any mismatch between traditional lecturing in the medieval age and lecturing in the contemporary university classroom?
Q3. How can teachers nowadays perform an effective lecture in today's hybrid lecture- based classroom?

9.2 Medieval Pedagogy

Lecture-based instruction has been the cornerstone of pedagogy. It allows teachers and instructors to enlighten students' minds and mould their thinking through the top-down transfer of knowledge. Educators refer to this instructional model as the "sage on the stage" (Lowe, 2011), "didactic learning" (Cottrell, 2007), or simply "teacher-centred" pedagogy. (Alexander & Winne, 2012) This typical instructional model has initiated an environment that supports academic learning since students listen to and work with their teacher. (Roger & Kutnick, 1992) As for the teacher, he or she had always been compared to the medical doctor, and indeed, the person who would bring learners to the birth of learning. (Buckenmeyer, 2009)

In the medieval age, textbooks have been widely used because they were regarded as the main source of knowledge and mentorship. The great majority of them were deployed in the faculties of theology and law. The first European university appeared in Bologna, where a great teacher called Irnerius (1088-1125) instructed Roman Law and attracted students from all over Europe. Most of the students that attended his lectures were ordinary people, and they were older learners serving as administrators for kings and princes; moreover, they were so excited to acquire more knowledge about Law in order that they might apply it in their jobs and occupations. (Duiker & Spielvogel, 2016) This view is endorsed by Toswell (2017), who argues that

> Students studied law because that gave them a very solid livelihood; they completed the studium generale because it gave them a good pragmatic education from which they could pursue law; they studied medicine to become medical professionals; and they studied theology if they wanted preferment in the Church. They did not aspire to think deep thoughts; they aspired to acquire posts with good remuneration and benefits. (p. 88)

The chapter has the potential to contribute with deep thoughts to the interconnectedness of art and pedagogy -- the way art, in general, and painting, in particular, intertwines with interpersonal communication as manifest in the lecture-based classroom. Interpersonal communication is inevitable in lecture-based instruction as it involves the swap and exchange of information, skills, thoughts and opinions between teachers and their students. Repeatedly, both of them alternate in the role of speaker and listener -- though all of them do not necessarily get "equal time. (McIntosh et al., 2008) My major premise is that artists are like teachers in as much as they are so capable of communicating their messages persuasively and intelligibly. Artists have by no means concerned themselves with the best transfer of knowledge and with the generation as well as the reception of information by others. They captured the strengths and weaknesses of ancient pedagogies, making them accessible to practitioners in all subjects and disciplines. Let us uncover these strengths and weaknesses in association with lecturing.

9.3 The Pros and Cons of Lecturing

Lecture-based instruction is an approach to teaching that endeavors to impart new knowledge to an audience about a particular subject. Because it was viewed as the sole method of effective instruction, lecture-based instruction allocated power to the teachers and maximized their control over the educational setting (Mishra, 2005); it brings forth discipline and appreciated conduct; and it hones students' cognitive and verbal intelligence. Furthermore, it can provide students with theories, models and procedures of work in their explorations of a topic. (Olsen et al., 2010) In certain situations, it allows for enthusiasm and increases students' level of motivation. In other educational contexts, it encourages them to analyze texts, summarize them and revisit their common ground knowledge. Other merits of the lecture-based method of instruction have been expounded by Aggarwal (2001) as follows:

1) It is economical as it needs no apparatus and no laboratory. A large number of students can be taught at a time.
2) It saves time and covers syllabus in a limited time.
3) It is effective in giving factual information and in relating some of the thrilling anecdotes. The life stories of great adventurers, experimenters, investigators and thinkers can become very interesting and valuable talks by a teacher.
4) Lecturing makes the work of teachers very simple. They need not make elaborate arrangements.
5) A good lecture not only stimulates the students but also lingers long in their imagination. It motivates them to become good orators. (p. 116)

In the traditional lecture-based classroom, teachers have drawn on the projector to display multimedia teaching resources for their students, such as video and audio files, and multiple documents. Owing to their inability to write directly on the projector, teachers wrote on the chalkboard by which the interaction between them and their students could be achieved. (Shi et al., 2018). The social interactions built in the classroom and the top-down or bottom-up communication can reveal a clash or a dialogue (Rymes, 2016) between teachers and their students.

However, lecture-based instruction has recently proven less efficacious because it does not involve all students and fosters the spirit of collaboration among them. For example, in the traditional lectures, the student often takes a largely passive role, and there is little opportunity for active learning such that the learner can engage with the subject matter being presented. (Fry et al., 2003) This is echoed by Zeng et al. (2020), who posit that traditional lecture-based learning is generally considered to induce passivity and compliance as it focuses on a one-way transfer of knowledge.

The cons of the lecture-based method of instruction have been developed by van Dijk and Jochems (2002) in an engineering class; they have found that a change from the traditional teaching approach in lectures towards a more interactive approach can be considered beneficial to students. Another disadvantage created by the lecture-based method of instruction is that the lecture and the textbook become the major delivery system of information for students who are required to listen and read in order to sit for exams in their respective universities. The latter, as people know them today – with students, faculty staff, departments, degrees and certificates, were products of the High Middle Ages.

Derived from the Latin word "universitas", meaning a guild or corporation, the term university alludes either to a corporation of teachers or a corporation of students. Medieval universities were educational guilds or corporations that gave birth to literate and qualified individuals (Duiker & Spielvogel, 2016), and these individuals made excellent contributions in art, science and literature. For some, Al-Qarawiyyine (also written Al-Karaouine), founded in Fez in 859 AD by a lady named Fatima al-Fihriya, is regarded as the oldest degree-granting university. (Sasnett & Sepmeyer, 1966; Weingarten, 2021; Kiwan, 2023) This prestigious Moroccan university had concentrated on the Islamic and religious sciences before it expanded to include other disciplines (e.g., mathematics and astronomy) and foreign languages such as French and English.

9.4 The Pedagogical Functions of Art

What can art tell us about lecture-based instruction and the medieval university classroom? Questions like these have troubled artists and painters almost in every part of the globe. Some years ago, Elliot Eisner advanced a thesis which states that the improvement of education is made possible not only by understandings promoted through the scientific method, but also those promoted through methods that are deeply rooted in the arts. (Eisner, 2009) When artists represent the system of education using oils and the paintbrush, form and the position, colours and propinquity, they unmask the complexity of education and consequently show a penchant for literacy and learning by stressing which teaching methodologies fit therein; more precisely, they encompass the educational arena with a critical and artistic sense so as to get all stakeholders to respond appropriately to any pitfalls. Their creative works open up new horizons for teachers to perform their jobs efficiently; and likewise, they are prone to raise students' awareness of the numerous challenges set in front of their teachers and instructors. It has been claimed by the Greek philosopher and polymath Aristotle that

> Essentially the form of art is an imitation of reality; it holds the mirror up to nature. There is in man a pleasure of imitation, apparently missing in lower animals. Yet the aim of art is to represent not the outward appearance of things, but their inward significance. (qtd. in Durant, 2022, p. 67)

Artists are more likely to paint, for instance, halls where lectures and courses take place, the design of the classroom, desks and chairs, the board utilized in teaching, social interactions between learners and their teachers, as well as the methods of explanation and edification. Such representation of the nuts and bolts of the educational system was feasible solely because artists themselves were literate people, who enjoyed inimitable feelings and inner perceptions about pedagogy and education. Put differently, artists have possessed discerning eyes and critical attitudes regarding optimal methods of learning and instruction. Attitudes here designate the way artists take advantage of their paintings to highlight their critical perspectives, the way they evaluate teachers and students' performances, how they depict classroom events and negotiate ideas in the classroom setting. Paintings were therefore used "to describe, illustrate, represent, show, the world." (Moroni & Lorini, 2020, p. 2)

"The Anatomy Lesson" of Dr. Nicolaes Tulp (1593-1674) is one stark example that illustrates the artist's preoccupation with the way knowledge ought to be disseminated to learners. Rembrandt has painted seven surgeons and the physician Nicolaes Tulp in 1632. The viewer could observe that learning about human anatomy necessitates concentration and wakefulness in the anatomy theatre; so learners can gain more insights into this field of work. Dr. Nicolaes Tulp's pose, as noted by Schulpbach (1982), is that of a man who is speaking to teach, and the members of the guild are listening to learn. Besides teaching by demonstration, the painting created a realistic representation of an anatomy lesson and abandoned the traditional formal and stiff arrangement of figures. (Ijpma et al., 2006)

"Scholars at a Lecture" is another painting that elucidates the obstacles of the lecturing method of instruction and the inconsistent feelings it induces in a given audience. The painting was designed by the British painter and printmaker William Hogarth (1697-1764). Special of this drawing is that it introduces a group of scholars wearing the same uniforms and hats that are indicative of graduate students and western academia. The academic professor, (believed to be William Fisher, Registrar of Oxford), though a connoisseur in his subject, he appears tedious while delivering his lecture, "Datur Vacuum" (A vacuum / leisure is granted). Around him stand a few students, who demonstrate a wide range of responses to the lecture in their caricatured faces: vacuity, boredom, indifference, amazement, doubt, distrust – every imaginable reaction but real interest. (Shesgreen, 1973) Arguably, the painting foregrounds the human dispositions that accompany the process of listening for a long time in the classroom sphere.

To better fathom the assets of the lecture-based method of instruction and its shortcomings, let us probe into a painting (consider Figure 9.1) by the Italian painter Laurentius de Voltolina; the drawing features in a virtually unknown manuscript, and it displays a medieval teacher, Henricus de Alemannia, in the process of lecturing to a group of students.

Figure 9.1: "Liber ethicorum" des Henricus de Alemannia
Staatliche Museen zu Berlin, Kupferstichkabinett / Jörg P. Anders
[Public Domain Mark 1.0]

Professor Henricus was an outstanding Professor, who excelled in the field of law, and he had composed his research in a treatise. The drawing, entitled "'Liber ethicorum' des Henricus de Alemannia", where he appears sitting engaged in teaching and lecturing, has become an ideal image of a medieval university lecture and one of the earliest concrete pictures of a university classroom.

> The image shows Henricus sitting at a cathedra, or lectern, reading passages to his students at the University of Bologna, one of the great medieval centers of learning whose faculty included the great poets Dante and Petrarch and the famous astronomer Nicholas Copernicus. (Austin, 2015, p. 21)

The coloured manuscript at hand harks back to the 1350s; it presents a heavily bearded lecturer seated at a podium reading aloud. (Hansen & Curtis, 2017) This was the norm because lecturers were viewed as readers that provide commentary on a variety of texts. At the front, an old student, most likely an advanced bachelor serving as the teacher's assistant, stands before the entire class.

9.5 Methods of Analysis

My analysis of the drawing builds on MDA -- a method of analysis that flourished widely in the interdisciplinary scholarship of Critical Discourse Analysis (CDA). MDA was proposed by Kress and van Leeuwen (2006); both have attributed representational, interpersonal, and compositional meanings to the critical reading of visual images. Like linguistic structures, visual structures include visual representational processes within and are closely bound up with participant roles and specific circumstances. When demystifying the interpersonal metafunction of paintings, the researcher should investigate the relationship between the visual representational processes and the viewer. This relationship can be explored further through visual cues such as facial expressions, gazes, gestures, the angle (i.e., is it horizontal or vertical?), all of which contribute to the level of engagement by the viewer. Finally, the compositional metafunction specifies the extent to which the visual and verbal elements accomplish a sense of coherence in the whole unit that requires the study of the page layout.

9.6 Findings

The analytical readings and interpretations that the viewers can give to Voltolina's painting hinge not only on their cultural identities but also on their situated knowledge. Situated knowledge means that there is no one truth waiting to be discovered; that approximately all forms of knowledge are situational, marked by the contexts in which they are produced, by their specificity, limited location and partiality. (England, 2014) Every person has a unique perspective about classroom discourse that embraces visual images and illustrations, yet most of the time, these perspectives are influenced by people's educational and cultural backgrounds. External influences, such as these, tend to forge their points of view and understanding of the world. (Suen & Suen, 2019) This holds true for the painting in question since problems of interpretation arise, especially in the identification of gender, the topic of the lecture, learners' age, nationalities, and their academic levels.

The detailed commentaries accompanying the painting help somehow disambiguate the obscured information. They are designed not to replace the painting but to support the understanding of it. The overall aim is to enable the viewers to make associations and draw analogies between texts in the present and the past, guiding them in the meantime to spot similarities and differences in higher education. Because of this, the interpretation of the painting requires of them to look deeply at the semiotic aspect of the text and check its pertinence and significance to their university lives. In this chapter, I conceive the term text as a visual phenomenon that can be seen, read, analyzed, and even interpreted. Any text is said to include several components, such as words, images, colours, posture, as well as design elements in its composition. When they are capable of relating it to their university lives and detecting its meanings and implications, the painting becomes more meaningful and worthwhile for teachers, researchers and twenty-first-century viewers.

A glance at the painting indicates that it concerns a university classroom of the medieval age. The classroom looks small and not overcrowded as it includes about 24 students of either gender: males (n=19) and females (n=5). All these students range from young undergraduates to greybeard. At least there is one student who is taking notes, some who are following the instructor in their own textbooks, and others who are dozing or talking to their peers. The authority of the teacher could be seen in the privileged position from which he lectures and his outfit, which is usually worn by scientists and sages of the ancient times.

Accordingly, the classroom setting introduces two social actors with different characteristics, features and qualities. The first social actor vehicles understanding and affability towards his audience. He is completely absorbed in his work and dissecting the educational environment attentively. He looks serious and firm on account of his very focused gaze, betraying scientific integrity and commitment to the teaching profession. The second social actors look somewhat inconsistent, scattered in terms of characters, gaze and conduct: there is the diligent student who maintains eye contact with the teacher, the motivated who struggles for more insights and understanding, the exhausted who is unable to catch up with the pace of the lecture, the drowsy that succumbed to lethargy as well as the pensive. As for the event, it revolves around a traditional lecture that can be described as interesting and simultaneously tiresome owing to the discordant reactions given by the students. Table 9.1 showcases the characteristics of the social actors and events that are foregrounded in Voltclina's painting:

Table 9.1: The characteristics of the social actors and event

Social actors and event	Characteristics
The teacher	- Firm; steadfast; calm; in control; focused; wise; patient
The students	- **Group 1:** attentive; diligent; focused; excited for learning; patient - **Group 2:** pensive; indifferent; drowsy; impatient
The lecture	- interesting - tiresome

In line with inclusive education that seeks to promote a context wherein "learning for all" is achieved (Sheehy, 2005, p. 2), the students who are occupying the front seats, more precisely in the first row, appear more attentive than their peers sitting at the rear of the classroom. Along with the students of the second row (and with the exception of one in a pensive mood), they all get engaged in the lecture. Their bottom-up gaze connotes esteem and admiration for the teacher and a strong desire to imbibe knowledge from him. In the third and fourth rows, most of the students show no interest in the lecture. They are either socializing or dozing due to physical and mental fatigue. Apparently, their mutual talks do not impede the teacher from carrying on his lecturing work on account of his vocation as a communicator, enlightener and edifier. That is, he is neither nervous nor angry, but rather still and with the patience of the job.

What is eye-catching is that four students are brought adjacent to the teacher; they are distinguished from the rest of the class to underscore their preeminence and to accentuate their self-autonomy and assiduity. This "preferred reading" (Hall, 1980) is endorsed by the teacher's facial expression and steady gaze established in a horizontal way to involve approximately all the students sitting at the front seats. One way to account for his stillness and decision to ignore disruptive behaviour is that the teacher owned the stamina, which was cultivated from a long teaching and lecturing experience. Another interpretation could be that students in the medieval university at Bologna wielded agency in as much as they periodically chose their teachers and even pay for their learning. (Rait, 1912) Hence, Voltolina's drawing

> Created the context that we will see today in having a professor standing at the front of a room, speaking to students who were supposed to listen and remember. Of note, some of these depictions, seemingly to illustrate realism, see student figures who are dozing if not asleep. (Bishop, 2021, p. 162)

Considering the concept of paratext, those textual elements that surround or frame the text, namely the subtitle (Martin & Ringham, 2006), the painting proffers us an idea about the place of traditional lecturing in the fourteenth century, which was a formal setting necessitating a specific code of behaviour, adherence to certain classroom etiquette, conformity to university regulations and regular attendance. Sometimes the place was the private house of the doctor, or a school rented for that purpose. In the case of an exceptionally popular professor whose students could not be crowded in any ordinary room, a public building or an open space in the city is said to have been borrowed for the same purpose. (Rashdall, 2010)

The representational metafunction of the painting resides in that it proposes a typical model of an ancient classroom discourse with all its basic ingredients. This discourse rests on the potential of lecturing to enhance learning, for it is, regardless of its shortcomings, amenable to literacy, cultivation and knowledge. By conceptualizing the lecture-based class and centring the teacher's character, the painter provides possible social interactions in the medieval university classroom, different learning situations, along with various models of behaviour that would shape higher education in many years to come: what university teachers experience today in their online and offline classrooms could be easily spotted in Voltolina's painting.

Coherence is crystallized amidst the frames of the painting. It evinces clearly in the paratext, the apparels of the teacher and the students, colours, and the fashion in which the educational space was sculpted and partitioned. Conventionally, the biggest space is reserved for the teacher, from whom students derive their knowledge and enthusiasms and at whose feet (not always though metaphorically) the students sit. (Hamlyn 2014) The books stretched out either on the teacher's lectern or over students' desks pinpoint that knowledge is made accessible through textbooks and printed materials. Thus, information was generated both from oral and written communication. The multiple metafunctions of the painting and their associated meanings are summarized in Table 9.2 here below:

Table 9.2: The metafunctions of the painting and their associated meanings

Metafunctions of the painting	Associated meanings
Representational	- Medieval classroom; university lecture; formal educational setting
Interpersonal	- Social interactions between students; teacher-students rapport; gaze (bottom-up and top-down) - Wakefulness vs. indifference; interest and lack of interest
Compositional	- Paratext; coherence; apparels, division of the classroom space - Colours (yellow, white, blue, green, red, black) - Objects (lectern, open books, desks and chairs, etc.)

The interpersonal dimension of the painting can be located in the different ways it enthrals the contemporary viewers and provokes their imagination to conjure up the university classroom of the medieval age. As a result, the viewer's gaze seems not fixed on a certain dimension of the painting but rather dispersed across the entire physical classroom that stresses multiple views, gesticulations, learning positions and talks of the students. The continuities and similarities of colour (i.e. yellow, red, green and black, blue), the visual shape of clothing and the open textbooks, are allusive to the symmetrical units of meaning that have to be extracted from the painting. In some sense, these elements are interlinked and inseparable; they are neither autonomous nor discrete since they work together to engender an overall impression of the medieval university classroom at the University of Bologna in Italy.

The central vector of representation here is not the word but the image that makes the painting highly evocative and expressive, merely because it emphasizes certain aspects of the art of lecturing and eclipses others. For example, the contemporary viewer does not know the titles of the textbooks used either by the teacher or his students, whether it is a morning or an afternoon lecture, the key concepts and definitions highlighted, etc. Consequently, the elements that are brought into focus have been called by Halliday (2004) "the theme" -- the point of departure for the message of communication; whereas, the elements that follow suit have been referred to as "the rheme." Compared to lecturing, which can be considered the focal theme of the painting as it is geared towards introducing new information, enlightening the students and emphasizing the wisdom and the forbearance of the teacher, students' chat, indifference and drowsiness can be regarded as the rheme because they are not only irrelevant to but also inappropriate for their successful learning.

9.7 Discussion

One of the findings of this study is that the lecture-based method of instruction does not appeal to all students; it does not cater to their expectations and aspirations. The students chatting and those dosing reveal that the lecturer encountered difficulties in reaching out to every single student. However, the students who are wakeful and attentive to the lecture present an opposite view that attaches learning and efficiency to the lecture-based method of instruction. Their diligence and concentration are due mainly to their resolution probably to become teachers and professors. That is, these students fell in love with learning, and they studied to become professors in the University of Bologna. (Toswell, 2017) In other words, their motivations were very likely the motivations of students today: fiscal and professional.

Another finding is that when teachers lecture, they might receive a plethora of responses from their students. In fact, all these responses oscillate between interest and indifference; teachers ought to anticipate various styles of learning and behaviours that cannot be disengaged from the educational sphere. The teacher's teaching style, if it does not match the students' learning styles, can lead to passivity, boredom and sometimes to occasional disruptive behaviour. This is why some students in the drawing have lost concentration and become distracted. When they become distracted, they unhesitatingly turn into a distraction for their diligent and studious peers. Teachers are thus entailed to consider students' learning styles when designing a lecture as previous research has found out that the teaching styles that align with learning styles can positively affect students' performances. (Lindsay, 1999) This is confirmed by Entwistle and Tait (1990), who contend that students prefer the teaching style that matches their conception of learning. If they believe that learning is memorizing facts, students vastly prefer traditional lectures; if they believe learning is building understanding, they prefer methods requiring them to be active. In this way, the lecture-based method of instruction has proven more suitable, especially for students who are auditory-oriented because they rely on speaking and listening as their preferred strategy for learning and processing information. By contrast, visual or tactile learners might experience exasperation and humdrumness when exposed to this style of teaching.

Significantly, the painting illustrates the close historical links between the scholarship of discovery and the scholarship of teaching and learning. (Nordkvelle, 2017) The scholarship of discovery is demonstrated by the teacher's open book that seemingly provides insight and wisdom. Whereas, the scholarship of teaching and learning is rendered by the partial or full attention students give to their professor. Furthermore, the painting exhibits that women were able to attend lectures in the medieval age and that learning was not exclusive to men. Women could talk freely to each other, take part in discussions and play vital roles in learning alongside their male compatriots. The arrangement of the classroom seats, its row style, carries signposts for teachers to supervise students' work and ensure that they are focused It is crystal clear that the painting instructs (Moroni & Lorini, 2020); it provides directions on how to do lecturing in higher education. Also, it projects the medieval university classroom as an arena of diversity and difference par excellence since both genders co-existed peacefully and were not discriminated against.

With respect to the colours chosen to embellish the painting, they fulfill several functions. (Kress & van Leeuwen, 2002) Starting with "the ideational" function, the white headcover denotes the teacher and underlines his unique identity. The green colour of the floor is a marker of intellectual growth and unpretentiousness. It represents peace, harmony and togetherness. The red and blue colours of students' headcovers evoke the idea of passion for learning and their inclination towards the lecture. The yellow colour suggests insights, knowledge and edification. The colours of the painting are therefore used to convey an "interpersonal" meaning." They can be and are used to do things to or for each other. Ultimately, colour can function at a "textual" level. In the medieval university classroom, the colour of the lectern, windows, the door, the floor and rows, on the one hand, distinguishes them from others situated in commonplace buildings, while on the other hand, creating unity and coherence within the same classroom; so colour can help create coherence in visual images as well.

Last but not least, the painting demonstrates that learning was not restricted to verbal communication as it involves other skills such as note-taking, reading, listening, and debating. Put differently, learning is dependent upon the teacher's communicative competence to tell stories and discuss quotes, raise complex questions and invite the students to think critically and creatively. It is assumed that Henricus' stories would be today taped, streamed or even exposed to reiterating practices of the "student-response-system"; we could even imagine students being invited to create digital stories in order to engage with the puzzles of legal ethics that were Professor Henricus' specialty. (Jamissen et al., 2017) Thus, the painting transfers given elements to a new learning / teaching context, a process which has been described as "Recontextualization." (Reisigl & Wodak, 2009) The most salutary advantage of this dynamic transfer is that it allows the contemporary viewer to question and ponder upon the affinities and disparities between contemporary and medieval lecture-based instruction.

9.8 Challenges and Recommendations

Among the challenges that teachers encounter while drawing on the lecture-based method of instruction in the twenty-first century university classroom, we can mention distraction and boredom. When the lecture begins, students are more likely to maintain a high level of attention, yet as the teacher proceeds on for more talk, some of them might feel less interested and frustrated. Sometimes, excessive lecturing leads to confusion and weariness, and the result is that students turn less passionate about their learning, which exacerbates the phenomenon of disruption and absenteeism in classes.

It is fair to say that the lecture-based method of instruction is an arm of double facets; it can enhance several skills, such as active listening, synthesizing and summarizing. Likewise, it scaffolds students' critical reflections and prepares them to be good public speakers and orators. Nevertheless, it is deemed as boring and does not stimulate students to develop reasoning skills. (Wan, 2014) In some contemporary universities, the lecture-based method of instruction is allotted more prominence compared to group or team work. To illustrate, when faced with a choice, the majority of students would favour lecture-based learning over team learning. (Opdecam & Everaert, 2019) This is why some researchers have recently inaugurated what is called interactive lecturing since it is more fruitful and is able to conduce meaningful learning. (Van Dijk & Jochems, 2002; Fyrenius et al 2005; Barkley & Major, 2018; Linsenmeyer, 2021) Besides, it can greatly help teachers bypass the challenges of handling large classrooms. (Nagmoti, 2020)

In such a novel approach to teaching and learning, teachers can deliver lectures effectively and involve students through a series of questions and answers so as to i) impart interest in them, ii) lead them to overcome monotony and indifference, and iii) enhance their intellectual growth. That being the case, the interactive lecture-based method of instruction is capable of minimizing the classroom distractions that impede students' success in higher education.

There is no doubt that Voltolina's painting has explicated the art of lecturing to professionals and non-professionals; it unveiled that teaching is really a daunting job demanding both resilience and self-sacrifice. To plan an effective interactive lecture in higher education, these recommendations are suggested:

1) Teachers should set up clear goals before every lecture;
2) They should incorporate audio-visual learning experiences with educational games and entertaining activities;
3) They should provide both the emotional and psychological back up for their students, especially the low-achievers;
4) They should monitor students' progress continuously through open and close-ended questions;
5) They should promote students' critical thinking skills, fostering both their self- efficacy and self-autonomy;
6) They should attune their ideas to satisfy students' higher needs and, in the meantime, live up to community standards.

9.9 Conclusion

Regardless of its deficiencies and shortcomings, the lecture-based method of instruction enables students to develop trust and esteem for their teachers. This trust and esteem, when they are lost, the whole enterprise of education collapses, and the learning outcomes remain unattained. If Laurentius de Voltolina is to draw his painting anew, he would add to it slight changes and new dimensions – probably PowerPoint Slides and some computers around the classroom setting; these pedagogical instruments have nowadays become essential to teaching and learning in the contemporary university classroom, which is getting larger and more diverse than ever before. The technology resources are now available to the teacher to implement his/her interactive lecture. As for the students, there are some who might feel drowsy and several others who will follow the pace diligently. Along with high-order skills, including but not limited to reasoning, inferencing, questioning and critical thinking, students' voices about the style of "Headlines" and "Blurbs" are fronted and meticulously explicated in the next chapter.

9.10 Further Readings

Cassidy, S. (2004). Learning styles: An overview of theories, models, and measures, *Educational psychology*, 24 (4), pp. 419-444, DOI: 10.1080/0144341042000228834

Entwistle, N. J. (1998). *Styles of learning and teaching*. London: David Fulton Publishers.

Kay, R., MacDonald, T. & DiGiuseppe, M. (2019). A comparison of lecture-based, active, and flipped classroom teaching approaches in higher education. *J comput high educ*, (31), pp. 449 - 471, https://doi.org/10.1007/s12528-018-9197-x

Loughlin, C., & Lindberg-Sand, A. (2023). The use of lectures: Effective pedagogy or seeds scattered on the wind?. *High educ*, (85), pp. 283-299, https://doi.org/10.1007/s10734-022-00833-9

Solomon, Y. (2020). Comparison between problem-based learning and lecture-based learning: Effect on nursing students' immediate knowledge retention. *Advances in medical education and practice*, (11), pp. 947-952, DOI: 10.2147/AMEP.S269207

9.11 Questions for Discussion

1) What are the advantages and shortcomings of the lecture-based method of instruction?

2) In your opinion, does this method address all styles of learning? Why (not)?

3) Based on Voltolina's painting, how can you describe classroom discourse in the medieval age?

4) Which semiotic aspects are foregrounded in the painting?

5) Do you agree that the lecture-based method is more suitable for auditory learners? Explain.

Part II:
NON-LITERARY TEXTS

Chapter 10

STUDENTS' VOICES ABOUT "HEADLINES AND BLURBS"

> **Highlights:**
> - *Most of headlines are pungent, concise and short.*
> - *They are written with big font and uppercase to grab readers' attention.*
> - *Several stylistic tropes such as ellipsis, emotive language and collocations are integral to the language of blurbs.*
> - *Another stylistic feature of headlines and blurbs is intertextuality.*
> - *These non-literary texts can be informative and persuasive.*

10.1 Introduction

This chapter, which is more likely to appeal to students aspiring to learn more about Genre and Language, Media Discourse and Composition Writing, draws an analogy between the stylistic features of "headlines" and the language features of "blurbs." To this end, some excerpts have been extracted from students' critical essays that were drafted in the Stylistics course. Whereas the headlines chosen grapple with the question of migration and refugees, the blurb in question addresses the pleasure of poetry reading. The chapter seeks to bring to the fore the potential aspects of meaning raised by the students in the Stylistics classroom. For the sake of clarification, we shall call the four students: Student A, Student B, Student C and Student D. Before shifting into their reflections on the blurb, it is fundamentally important that we scrutinize how they have approached the style of headlines.

10.2 The Language of Headlines

Formulating headlines is not as easy as it may appear to be. Headlines are characterized by being short, pungent and catchy; hence, captivating headlines can be more crucial to the reader than the story or the main news themselves. As Applegate (2005, p. 41) notes, "The best headlines appeal to the reader's interests or desires." Let us examine how Student A viewed style in the following headline: NEW NEIGHBORS, NEW CONSIDERATIONS.

Student A

> In English language, most headlines are short, pungent and concise. Take for example the following headline: "New Neighbors, New Considerations." It is a sentence fragment taken from an article by Henry Alford in The New York Times, published on October 4, 2017. The headline introduces how Syrian refugees adapt to change. This headline contains a nominal structure comprising two nouns and two descriptive adjectives alluding to a current situation. The writer resorted to parallelism and repetition to emphasize that refugees are turning into neighbors in the host land. Everyone is entailed to accept and welcome them. This is clearly expressed in the use of the word "Neighbors." The presence of the comma is elusive because it denotes that some words have been deliberately omitted to provoke the reader's thoughts. Probably there is an omission of the verb "requires" or "necessitates"; so the headline would run as follows: New Neighbors Requires New Considerations.

The stylistic reflection provided by Student A showcases that the style of headlines invariably takes into account the sentence length, its grammatical structure and formal aspects such as parallelism and repetition, its graphology, and finally, ellipsis. Student A was capable of figuring out the omitted words that have been substituted for the comma and obtaining a complete picture of the purport of the headline regardless of its brevity and conciseness. What is eye-catching is that Student A has put the headline in its proper context by mentioning authorship, the newspaper where it featured and the meaning intended by the term "Neighbors." The same headline was examined by another student, whom we shall refer to as Student B. Albeit the focus was the same, the interpretation varied since the students apprehend style in different ways. What is style for one is not necessarily style for another.

Student B

> Headlines are called the display window of the newspaper/article. The first thing the reader notes is the headline of the article and only then decides whether to read it or not; therefore, headlines are among the most important components of the piece of writing in the journalistic discourse. Every writer has his/her own style of writing which distinguishes them from others. The aforesaid headline is verbless as it

contains no verbs. As mentioned before, there are some words that are missed out, a stylistic trope called ellipsis, meant to capture the reader's attention. Most newspapers now use headlines that say what has to be said in a minimum of words.

They are sometimes difficult to understand, because they are written in a special and highly sophisticated manner. Strikingly, headlines often include a parallel structure, which means using the same pattern of words to show that two or more ideas have the same level of importance. Headlines concisely state the main idea of text and indicating the nature of the article. Briefly stated, headlines are an advertisement for the news story.

A glimpse of the analysis provided by student B reveals that the style of headlines inevitably involves ellipsis, conciseness and parallelism. The ability to say more ideas in a minimum of words demonstrates not only a good command of language but also prowess in terms of style. The choice of vocabulary and lexical items can be considered in any discussion of headlines. Writers often manipulate vocabulary to embellish headlines and create various stylistic imprints. Sometimes, and in so far as Schmitt and Schmitt (2020, p. 202) are concerned, 'they do this by exploiting lexical ambiguity." This means that there is more than one reading and interpretation of the headline, and that the meaning of words and phrases are quite misleading, especially when verbal structures are discarded. When lexical ambiguity is brought to the fore, the interest for reading the story grows and the curiosity of knowing its details increases.

The third headline that is worth examining is IMAGINING REFUGIA. (Van Hear, 2017) Why should we bother ourselves with analyzing the stylistics of this previous headline? Unlike its counterpart indicated above, this headline does not involve parallelism, yet it is still awash with ellipsis, which is triggered by the presence of the gerund "Imagining." The latter inculcates vagueness and ambiguity into the headline because it sounds more like a noun than a verb. Personally, what I appreciated about the students' analyses is their ability to make associations between the headlines they interpret and their common ground knowledge or **schema** that relates to the mental structures in their minds in which they have stored all the information gathered from the world around them. (Aubrey & Riley, 2022) Note for instance, how this student links "Refugia" to "Utopia", and how she tends to question every lexical/linguistic choice because, at least for her, it is purposeful and pragmatic. Here is a short analysis of the headline IMAGINING REFUGIA as presented by the third student:

Student C

When looking at headlines' formation, one can notice that they are usually composed of a concise, short and succinct piece of text. Obviously, the typography of headlines is what distinguishes them from other genres of texts. This serves to hook the readers and give them a quick glimpse of the content of the news story. This critical reflection describes the linguistic features of the headline, "Imagining Refugia", and it provides a reasonable interpretation about the usage of such concentrated language.

The headline at hand seems to combine two terms belonging to different word classes: "Imagining" and "Refugia." The first, which features as a gerund, means to constitute a mental image of a thing that does not exist – that which is not real. The second, however, is a common irregular noun, referring to a geographical area, yet it has positive overtones. By bringing these two words together, the writer endeavors to attract the attention of readers and arouse their curiosity about the content of the news story. What is stunning is that this time the gerund does not occur within larger sentence constructions where it can serve either as a subject or an object, for here it is attached to one Latin word, "Refugia" (plural form of refugium), which makes meaning incomplete. Following this claim, the writer might have relied on the creativity of the readers to guess and deduce the missing part.

On another perspective, precisely the choice of words adopted by the writer, one can construe the strong impact the word 'Refugia' has on readers' minds. Astonishingly, this particular word rhymes perfectly with 'Utopia', an ideal place describing an imaginary society in which everything is perfect. Utopia is a beautiful land that is devoid of any discrimination, earthly problems or societal complications. We can refer to it simply as paradise. Hence, one can infer from the choice of this specific term a stark example of intertextuality and allusion that direct the thinking of readers to a place of dreams and perfection. By the same token, the other word preceding it cannot be replaced, let alone be omitted; it cannot be substituted for any other synonym as it is a unique term, prompting people to use their imagination properly and conjecture happy life in this beautiful place. When accounting for the intralinguistic and extralinguistic context, one can easily realize that the news story concerns the struggles and ongoing afflictions which refugees experience in their move towards their utopian dreams.

Like her peers, Student C concentrated on the sentence length, the stylistic makeup of the headline, its typography and word choice. She was clever as she moved beyond the superficial meaning of the headline to think and speak of the aspirations of refugees when they leave their homelands for better life conditions. The most compelling aspect of her critical analysis lies in her capacity to point to Plato's utopian perception of the perfect land, depicted in his *Republic*. That this student managed to build rhyme between "Refugia" and "Utopia" clearly attests to her prudence as far as her style is concerned; so if Student A insisted on accepting, respecting and welcoming the new neighbours (i.e., the refugees), Student B was limited to the linguistic / semantic properties, and he evoked some general aspects such as parallelism, artistry in terms of language use, ellipsis, nominalization and conciseness that are more likely to figure in any newspaper headline.

Nevertheless, the stylistic analysis penned by Student C reveals that acute specifications and the power of imagination ought to forge any close examination, reading or reflection upon style. Besides being so creative in the articulation of her ideas, this particular student spotted a significant literary theory (i.e., intertextuality) by making word associations and drawing inferences; she used her imagination skills when she built a mental image about the new place where refugees can settle and dwell. It is, in so far as Student C is concerned, "a beautiful land that is devoid of any discrimination, earthly problems or societal complications." That is, it is a land of dreams, peace and extreme joy. We can refer to it as "paradise lost."

Although I give students the freedom to choose which aspects to cover in the stylistic analysis of headlines, I think only a few of them embark on interpreting these texts from a critical perspective by questioning form, hidden meanings, implicatures, and the overall impressions it triggered in them as readers. (Acim, 2021) I always remind them that they are not required to reach the same conclusions when approaching the pragmatic aspects, yet it is mandatory that they arrive at the same results as far as the semantic level of meaning is concerned. Since they have different abilities, skills and learning preferences (Echaore-McDavid, 2006; Airey & Tribe, 2005; Wellington & Ireson, 2013) they also need to exhibit their own understanding of texts in the most optimal ways.

In light of what has been mentioned thus far, we can say that the focus of the students is primarily geared towards some layers of language like graphology, semantics and syntax, which are all central to style. In certain cases, their critical analyses tap into the pragmatic meanings of texts, as did Students A and C above. In fact, what they agree about is that headlines are all the time presented in big font and bloc letters. They are written with the uppercase to hook more readers and increase the newspapers' sales. Sometimes, the story can be very interesting and fascinating; however, it is not reached out, nor is it fully explored if the headline is poorly designed and crafted. Poor style would never engage readers; it will never spark their interest to purchase the newspaper and discover the purport of the news story told. If these students' viewpoints about the style of headlines vary, what will their peers think of the structure and function of the blurb?

10.3 A Blurb: "Poem in Your Pocket"

A blurb is that brief and exquisite statement found on the jacket of the book, and its primary objective is publicity. It is widely assumed that the blurb can be one of the most important aspects of the publishing industry since few words can sell one's book to readers or drive them away from it. (Showalter & Monroe, 2020) Almost like headlines, blurbs are informative and persuasive at the same time. They tend to contribute to the marketing of the book on a wide scale. Besides the use of sound patterning such as assonance and alliteration, publishers carefully choose the language and sentence structures of blurbs to make them coherent and organic.

Let us consider the following blurb:

> *Poem in Your Pocket* enables you to select a poem you love, tear it out neatly from this book, and carry it with you all day to read, be inspired by, and share with others – or keep to yourself. This innovative format features 200 classic and contemporary poems by more than 100 poets, from Shakespeare to Sylvia Plath, cleverly organized by theme. If you're feeling wistful, if you want to romance your lover, if you're celebrating the seasons, or if you just need a poem to get you through the day, this wonderful selection will help you spread the power of poetry or treasure it in private. (Bleakney, 2009)

What makes the style of the above-mentioned blurb quite special? Which functions does it perform? Is it informative or persuasive? Is it both? How does the writer invest on the levels of language to convey his meaning? Who is the author of the blurb? Who is the target audience? What is the overall theme of the blurb? Is there any room for metaphorical and proverbial expressions? This is what the fourth student aims to show in the following fully developed critical essay:

Student D

> Blurbs can be defined as promotional texts that accompany books. They have an informative function based on the content and the description of the book. Stylistics, as the most appropriate approach, examines the language of the blurb from a linguistic angle. As one of the most powerful instruments that define the success of the book, blurbs take

advantage of sensational words, which all appear to be more suitable for the automated recognition of feelings and human emotions. Every single term from it has the power to produce a lasting impact on the reader; so what are the main characteristics that enrich the blurb to fulfill its persuasive function? How do publishers in the book industry craft such exquisite and impressive discourse?

To start with, one can clearly observe that the language of this blurb, "Poem in Your Pocket", is engaging since the intent is to grab the full attention of the reader, and by extension, to accomplish its advertising mission. The writer of the above blurb has resorted to metaphorical language (i.e. a poem cannot be in a pocket) so as to evaluate, celebrate and praise the book. This is expressed in the first statement of the blurb: "Poem in Your Pocket" that has been italicized to direct readers to it. Furthermore, one may notice the use of hyperbole (overstatement and exaggeration) like "get you through the day"; "wonderful selection'; "celebrating the seasons", "spread the power", "treasure it." The purpose is certainly to express intensification, enthrall if not move as many readers as possible.

From the second reading, one is informed that this blurb selects only two renowned figures among more than a hundred poets; these two popular figures are "Shakespeare" and "Sylvia Plath", who are more likely to be recognized easily by the average reader. Besides, one might be skeptical as regards the author of this blurb. True, it can be a male or a female. However, upon scrutinizing the blurb's lexis and emotional vocabulary, one can conclude that the author is probably a female because women are claimed to be more interested in topics of romance and poetry than men. Women also are used to choosing carefully their words and expressions. Unlike men, they use more intensifiers and evaluative adjectives such as "wonderful" and "organized," but this claim, for some stylisticians, remains only a cliché.

In the blurb under scrutiny, the writer has employed a wide range of complementary words by insisting upon and (over)emphasizing the strengths of the book. Consider, for instance, the collocative constructions in "cleverly organized"; "wonderful selection"; "innovative format", etc. These lexical forms are abundantly used to proffer the book some weight and an extraordinary value. Moreover, cohesion is at stake; it is manifest not only in the consecutive repetitions of similar grammatical structures but also in the usage of personal referencing, which is commonly known as deixis. The person deictic "you" (n=9) refers to readers of all times and places. Proximal deictics (n=3), disguising in demonstrative referencing through determiners are taking center stage. Note for example "<u>this</u> book" / "<u>this</u> wonderful" /

"<u>this</u> innovative." According to linguists, referencing, and by implication deixis, plays an important role in making discourse clearer, more appealing and effective.

The clever usage of rhetorical moves engages the reader and empowers the book. What is striking is that the blurb sets several possibilities and conditions to involve all readers no matter what their interests, gender or concerns are. This is tacit in the domination of conditional forms introduced by the if-clause. To increase the sales of the book, enhance the advertised product at a wide scale, incentivize potential readers to immediately purchase it, the writer formulated a complex sentence of four dependent "if-clauses" and one main / independent clause.

To conclude, we may argue that the main function of this blurb is persuasion and not just information. The writer's purpose has been to elicit a positive feedback from readers, to influence their minds and thoughts through the use of emotive language. Proper nouns, adjectives, parallel grammatical structures, ellipsis alongside deixis, are all intended to persuade readers that the book in question ought to be treasured and saved like a coin in their pockets.

The commentary advanced by Student D on the blurb *Poem in Your Pocket* explains well the good inferencing and writing skills she has mastered in the Stylistics course. Almost every aspect of meaning has caught her full attention, which means that she reads the blurb with a critical mind while mulling over the linguistic choices considered consciously or unconsciously by the writer. This is a typical example of how students can build and structure their stylistic analyses and explorations of blurbs' language. A brief introduction to what a blurb is and its inherent connection and linkage to style seems desirable, in addition to two probing questions that can galvanize students to apprehend style sufficiently and more adequately. Here below, I suggest other workable measures for better planning, organization and drafting of any critical reflection on style and meaning in texts.

10.4 Practical Tips and Guidelines

Before they indulge in the stylistic debates about word choice, implicit and explicit meanings, the purpose of the blurb, its context and register, the nature of language employed, and whether this language is inclusive or exclusive of metaphors and symbols, students should devise the two questions and advance their ideas in an unbiased and consistent manner. As Rothstein & Santana (2011) note, the entire learning experience can be transformed if students, rather than teachers, assume responsibility by posing questions. The two questions suggested for the drafting of the stylistic analysis enable the students to profoundly explore the text and relate it to their personal lives. In so far as Francis (2016) is concerned, questions are the most instructional strategies that can provide the proper scaffolding to enlarge students thinking, understanding and application of knowledge.

After she had whetted the reader's appetite to read her thorough reflection on the blurb, Student D listed down some elaborate and exhaustive notes on its distinct characteristics, detailing its purpose and mission. It is evident that she scrutinized any rhetorical devices such as metaphors and hyperbole, that found a room in the blurb. Moreover, she highlighted their functions in the overall discourse. Later, she examined the most prominent lexical categories, namely proper nouns, intensifiers and adjectives, underscoring their vitality and significance to the blurb. Afterwards, she inquired about the social background and gender identity of the author as they are more likely to influence tremendously the formulation and reception of the blurb. Then, she cast some light on lexical and grammatical linking, which obviously holds the blurb together and gives meaning to it. The linking at hand is described by the student as cohesion, and it is eased by a whole galaxy of techniques like collocative patterns, repetitions and deixis.

In the end, Student D launched a recap of the objective of the blurb and proceeded to talk about response theory and the writer's (ideology) aim, which is, without a shadow of a doubt, to impress and impact on readers' minds and behaviour. The procedure of analysis proposed could be applied and adapted to the study of other texts, literary or non-literary. It works better when students work collaboratively in groups and brainstorm the most salient features of style. Their resolution to critique and systematically analyze style is in itself nothing but an exploration of meaning; it entails that the students describe, interpret and evaluate both the linguistic and non-linguistic environments where the texts were produced. This activity needs a good comprehension of texts, a mental effort, and an ability to transform the abstract interpretations into a concrete and well-organized reflection. This goes in conformity with Shanahan (2012), who believes that teachers should teach students to seek particular types of information when they read a text. They need to teach them how texts are organized or structured and how to use these organizational plans to remember or understand information effectively.

10.5 Conclusion

Headlines and blurbs are good examples where style merges writing with action. They are invariably used to incite readers to search for more ideas in newspapers and books. Some headlines can move the readers' hearts because they are snappy, while others can force them to take sides. Concerning blurbs, they play prominent roles either in increasing or decreasing the book sales. Indeed, such diverse functions, both of headlines and blurbs, are noteworthy in the four critical reflections initiated by the students, who were responsive to style and sensitive to the choices made by the writers at different formal and functional levels. The reflections not only reiterate that these students become so alive to the various levels of language where style operates, but they also account for their awareness of its intent and effect. This is why it seems relevant to expose the reader more to this persuasive dimension of the media discourse by listing down the principal rhetorical tropes reporters capitalize on in their news stories and opinion pieces.

10.6 Further Readings

Giovanelli, M. (2018). Pedagogical stylistics: A text world theory approach to the teaching of poetry. *English in education*, 44 (3), pp. 214-231, https://doi.org/10.1111/j.1754-8845.2010.01074.x

Jalilifar, A., Hayati, A., Moosavinia, S. R., & Jafar, D. (2016). A cross-cultural analysis of English Arabic blurbs: An investigation into generic structure and appraisal markers. *Teaching English language*, 10 (2), pp. 1-23, DOI: 10.22132/TEL.2016.53536

Ptashchenko, N. (2008). *Headline as a persuasive tool in publicistic discourse.* Norderstedt, Germany: GRIN Verlag.

Saxena, S. (2006). *Headline writing.* London: Sage Publications.

Valor, L. G. (2005). Advertising books: A linguistic analysis of blurbs. *IBERICA*, 10, pp. 41- 62, https://citeseerx.ist.psu.edu/viewdoc/download?doi=10.1.1.672.4951&rep=rep1&type=pdf

10.7 Questions for Discussion

1) What are the stylistic features of "headlines"?

2) In your opinion, why should readers read "blurbs" first before moving to the content of the book?

3) Are there any common linguistic traits between the style of "blurbs" and "headlines"?

4) Is the purpose of "headlines" all the time commercial? Explain.

5) Examine style in the following headlines:

HOW TO BUY HAPPINESS (RESPONSIBLY). (Lieber, 2020)
WHAT DO YOU THINK ARE THE SECRETS TO HAPPINESS. (Engle, 2021)
HAPPINESS WON'T SAVE YOU. (Senior, 2020)
HAPPINESS IS OTHER PEOPLE. (Whippman, 2017)
MONEY CAN BUY HAPPINESS – IF YOU KNOW HOW TO USE IT. (Marte, 2016)

6) How can you describe the language of the blurb below? Is it similar to "Poem in Your Pocket?" Explain.

> "No single book has captured the range of Edward Said's knowledge like *Power, Politics and Culture* In these twenty-nine interviews collected over the last three decades, Said addresses everything from Palestine to Pavarotti, from his nomadic upbringing under colonial rule to his politically active and often controversial life in America. Said's passion for literature, music, history and politics is everywhere apparent, confirming his status as one of the most thought-provoking and engaging thinkers of our time."

Chapter 11

RHETORICAL TROPES: "THE NEW YORK TIMES"

> **Highlights:**
>
> - *Discourse can be defined as the interaction of a text with its environment.*
> - *The juxtaposition of metaphors is neither random nor fortuitous.*
> - *Language has six functions: referential, emotive, conative, phatic, metalingual and poetic.*
> - *The NYT tends to manufacture consensus about topics such as Islam and Muslims in the realm of media.*
> - *The discourse of the NYT is rhetorical and persuasive.*

11.1 Introduction

This chapter assists undergraduate students interested in Discourse Analysis, Journalism and Rhetorical Studies to approach the media content from a critical lens. The employment and juxtaposition of figures of speech is not accidental because it demonstrates that writers constantly and consistently utilize a wide range of options from the linguistic repertoire not only to inform but to persuade their audience as well. My goal is to examine the rhetorical tropes considered, consciously or unconsciously, by the writers of the NYT in their text and talk of Islam and Muslim minorities. Foregrounding theory, which has been a keystone in Stylistics and literary theory, is adapted to dismantle the newspaper's complex and multifaceted meanings. First let us reflect again on the multiple functions of language.

11.2 The Functions of Language

Since antiquity, human beings have been so fascinated by the use of language and the art of speech. Style, among other linguistic features, has gained a succinct attention of readers and analysts alike. The choice of lexes, structures and other discursive devices, either for persuasion or information, has prompted a number of linguists to (re)question the functional side of language.

The publication of Michael Halliday's (1925-2018) *Introduction to Functional Grammar* (IFC) in 1985, marked a breakthrough in linguistics because it viewed language as a "social semiotic." According to Halliday, the central focus of language is to do something, the theory of SFL [Systemic Functional Linguistics] addresses what language does and how it is done. (Dong, 2006) Whereas some linguists have concentrated on determining the formal properties of language – language as langue/competence, being the code or system of abstract structures and rules common to speakers, others were committed to an investigation of what that language is used for. (Brown & Yule, 1983) In so far as Lock is concerned (2014), language has several functions other than modeling reality:

> Communication is usually offered as the major function with the semantic aspect of words conceived as the vehicle. But the prosody, the tempo, the pauses, the associated gestures, postures and facial expressions may be more informative than the words themselves. What is not said may be more revealing than the language used. (p. 34)

In a similar vein, the Russian formalist, Roman Jakobson (1896-1982), has produced a more detailed notion of the several functions of language by suggesting that any verbal communication involves at least six factors:

1) *Referential*: it refers to and conveys information about the world.
2) *Emotive*: it expresses the author's attitude towards their utterance (e.g., through choice of words or tone of voice).
3) *Conative*: it influences the hearer/reader (e.g., through requests or demands).
4) *Phatic*: it makes contact rather than conveys meaning: initiating, sustaining or closing communication.
5) *Metalingual*: it refers to the language code itself (e.g., to check on specific meanings).
6) *Poetic*: it focuses on the message for its own sake, emphasizing the linguistic qualities of the language used. (qtd. in Maybin & Swann, 2010, p. 45)

Almost like all modalities of discourse, newspapers' language is forged to vehicle information to people, yet information is not the only aim of newspapers because at the very crux of media in general is persuasion. The *raison d'être* for the newspapers, as Cull et al. (2003, p. 268) argue, is "persuasion, propaganda favoring a particular political view." Headlines, as we saw in the previous chapter, have a persuasive function as they are designed to grab the attention of the readers and interest them in reading the news story (or, in the case of front page headlines, in buying the newspaper), but they can also be written to influence the opinion of the public; so what is unique about the style of the journalistic discourse and in particular the NYT news stories and Op-Eds?

11.3 The Style of the Journalistic Discourse

Studies of language and style, or Stylistics and language, abound due to the multi- dimensional aspects of human discourse. Language is identified as 'an enabling device", which allows human beings frequently to articulate the sequence of choices, decisions, responses, acts and consequences that make up their lives. (Bradford, 1997, p. xi) Arguably, each genre uses a distinctive style of language – and each style is used in a different communication system (i.e., professional science, popular science) – and each represents and privileges, as well, a different but distinctive way to know the world and make claims about it. Journalistic style, for instance, has been referred to as an omnibus term comprising different stylistic patterns. (Rao, 2011)

The style of dailies varies from that used in periodicals. Styles used by national and regional dailies also differ in a remarkable way. While the former may use dignified and crisp language close to Standard English, the latter is more affected by geosocial language peculiarities. This means that journalists have developed formidable ways of addressing their readers. Sections pertaining to arts, women, sports and classified ads use special styles of text and talk, with a view to catering to the various readership segments. It is not surprising then that most newspapers maintain their own 'house style of guidelines.' (ibid.) Newspapers thus include multiple designs and styles of writing. Features and news stories look different from Editorials; Editorials are not similar in tone and voice to Op-Eds, and book reviews share uncommon properties with obituaries. The reception of these newspapers varies according to quality, style and sales.

11.4 Broadsheets vs. Tabloids

In terms of the style and format of newspapers, one can also differentiate between quality (broadsheets) and popular (tabloids) newspapers. Quality or broadsheet refers to the size of a newspaper, which is characterized by large sheets of newsprint. It also carries particular connotations of journalistic quality and seriousness of news coverage. Conversely, tabloids or popular newspapers have come to be associated with a more entertainment-oriented, sensationalistic, and colloquial style. (Sterling, 2009) This difference between either kind is summarized by Hughes (1989, pp. 131-2) in the following words:

Certain broad generalizations can be made about the news-style of the "quality" press as opposed to the "popular" press. The "popular" press relies on a sensational treatment of a small segment of the news, one which may be banal or momentous. This it achieves by emphasis on a few "stories" arranged hierarchically on the front page, with top priority given to "human interest" or rarity items. These are dramatized by large headlines, powerful emotive language and the impact of sizable, close-up photographs invariably "cropped" out of their original shape. Contrariwise, the "quality" paper attempts to give a more balanced and sober "spread" of news with emphasis on world events presented in neutral language, with smaller, rectangular photographs being used to create interest, but not drama.

As an American broadsheet, the NYT attempts to manufacture consensus about Muslim and Arab minorities in the realm of media, through a dexterous and an emotive language. On the grounds of its professionalism in print and digital news reporting, the NYT is still America's national newspaper of record; it is "a formidable institution with tremendous journalism muscle that has staying power, as well as the eyes and ears of decision-makers, the elite, and increasingly the ordinary public." (Usher, 2014, p. 8) In truth, the classification of the rhetorical tropes featured in the NYT news outlet helps the reader gain a new insight into its persuasive and ideology-based discourse.

11.5 Corpus

The Op-Eds (Opposite Editorials) and news stories considered for this rhetorical analysis have been retrieved from the digital archive of the NYT. The collection at hand ranges from 1997 to 2024, and it contains a total of 21 pieces with an average length of 1000 words. The selection process follows non-probability sampling, a research technique which does not involve random selection. This chapter paves the ground for understanding journalistic style and developing a comprehensive view of how opinions are structured and presented to the average or intellectual readers. It sheds light on the rhetoric permeating the discourse of the NYT since this discourse functions as a site for the exhibition of stylish writing and flamboyance.

11.6 Style as Motivated Options

In my rhetorical analysis of the NYT Op-Eds and news stories, I depart from the claim that says that journalistic discourse has unique ways of using language and appropriating it to fulfill various perlocutionary ends. Verdonk's (2002) conception of Stylistics is useful as long as it concentrates on the elements that stand out in a text -- those that seek to create a psychological impact on the potential readership. This is confirmed by Stockwell (2002), who maintains that some aspects of texts are commonly viewed as being more important or salient than others. Although this is partly a controversial issue, it is also largely a matter of the cues that the text provides. In literary and non-literary texts, persuasive techniques are always emphasized and called for because they seem to back up the rhetorical structure and intentional meaning of the text:

> In making a stylistic analysis we are not so much focused on every form and structure in a text as on those which stand out in it. Such conspicuous elements hold a promise of stylistic relevance and thereby rouse the reader's interest or emotions. In stylistics this psychological effect is called **foregrounding**, a term which has been borrowed from the visual arts. Such foregrounded elements often include a distinct patterning or parallelism in a text's typography, sounds, word-choices, grammar, or sentence structures. (emphasis is in Verdonk, 2002, p. 6)

Given that the NYT reporters write differently as everyone has his/her typical style of writing and reporting on day-to-day events, it seems adequately convenient to break off the NYT articles into several segments and small pieces, with the purpose of unpacking the stylistic as well as rhetorical devices that stand out. Applied to journalistic writing, the tools of a rhetorical / stylistic analysis, which is considered in this chapter, "provide a new approach to understanding the artistry, function, and meaning of a text." (Duke, 1990, p. 149) This analysis involves diagnosing the multiple ways in which writers endeavour to influence and persuade readers through their discursive, communicative and textual practices. There is no denying that the rhetorical texture and the stylistics of a work are not extraneous, cosmetic elements, but they make up its full essence, and consequently, determine whether the work itself persuades or just communicates.

The presence of certain rhetorical tropes is especially prominent in the discourse of the NYT. Though generally associated with canonical literature, grammatical parallelism (balancing ideas by putting them in a series), antithesis (contrasting ideas by directly opposing them linguistically), alliteration (repeating the initial sound of two or more words), and assonance (repeating the same vowel sound or more vowels), appear commonplace in this non-literary discourse. (Ryan, 1995)

11.7 Rhetorical Tropes

Upon investigating the rhetorical tropes of the NYT discourse, it was found that the writers invariably utilize multiple devices to impress upon and influence the minds of their readers. The metaphor, and its close friend, the simile, are commonly used. In fact, both tropes create a poetic impact through the prism of language that brings together ideas and images in unexpected conjunction. (Cameron, 2003) To attract the audience's attention, the writers of the NYT also dwell on ellipsis, anaphora, metonymy, regular neologisms, borrowings, intertextuality, the editorial "We", honorifics, antithesis and the like. These stylistic and rhetorical tropes (n=21) certainly arouse powerful feelings in people and stir up their thoughts, given the kind of gratification they instil into their intellects. I have italicized and sometimes underlined these tropes to enable the reader to localize them easily. Now let us examine the next excerpts from the NYT that fused these stylistic and rhetorical devices in different occasions:

- *Ellipsis*: it is an intentional deletion of some expressions which aim to economize the use of language, establish grammatical cohesion and stimulate readers to think outside the box. Martin (2009, p. 155) claims that ellipsis indicates "resources for omitting a clause, or some part of a clause or group, in contexts where it can be assumed." In the next excerpt, ellipsis is vehicled through the usage of the dash, which apparently marks a sudden transition in the idea expressed. While it can be argued that the NYT reporter has left out one subordinate clause (i.e. that are), he resolved to offer explanations and better clarify his point as concerns "traditional values":

    These marriages -- invariably arranged, and often forced -- have two chief motivations. One is to provide the foreign spouse with Norwegian residency rights under the "family reunification" provision of immigration law. The other is to resist integration by injecting into the European branch of the family a fresh dose of "traditional values" -- among them a hostility to pluralism, tolerance, democracy and sexual equality. ARRANGED MARRIAGES PREVENT INTEGRATION: A TRAP FOR MUSLIM WOMEN IN EUROPE (*The New York Times*. June 27, 2003).

- *Metaphor:* it is a figure of speech and a form of analogy that describes a subject by asserting that it is, on some point of comparison, the same as another otherwise unrelated object. In metaphors, comparisons and analogies are done without using words such as "like" and "as" [for more details, see Chapter 3]. In the following excerpt, the writer has used a metaphor when he noted that Shahana is a dream of the Democratic Club. Arguably, this image is stronger than the one built with the instrument of comparison for Aicha al-Adawiya, who is described as a "living legend":

> Ms. Sarsour decided long ago not to run for political office, realizing she could achieve more behind the scenes, she said. She is inspired by the work of Aicha al-Adawiya, 77, a Black Muslim leader and human rights activist whom Ms. Sarsour described as a "living legend"… "Shahana is someone that I dreamed about 10 years ago," Ms. Sarsour said. "*She's a dream of our Democratic Club*, manifested. HOW GROWING UP IN NEW YORK AFTER 9/11 SHAPED THESE MUSLIM LEADERS (*The New York Times*. September 10, 2021).

- *Intertextuality*: it designates the manner different texts reference or interact with other texts. Most of the time, such rhetorical device is carried out through a quotation, allusions or parody. As has been mentioned earlier (see also Chapter 6), this concept was introduced in the 1960s by the French critic Julia Kristeva, who was influenced by the Russian theorist Mikhail Bakhtin. Observes Stockwell (2007, p. 125), this rhetorical device can be applied to the prominent allusions made in one (non)literary work to another work, which "serve to produce counterpoint, continuity, or irony, or draw on authority, or increase artistic richness or resonance." Consider the next extract, which includes an intertext as the writer has inserted a quotation from the Quran to elucidate and account for the popular expression "inshallah" (lit. God willing), circulating widely among Muslim families and friends:

> When I was growing up, my family used the expression "inshallah" a lot. For Muslims, the term -- which translates to "If God wills" -- is auspicious: If you want something to happen, you should say "inshallah" before you say anything else about it. The Quran says as much in its eighteenth chapter, Surah Al-Kahf. "And never say of anything, 'Indeed, I will do that tomorrow,' except [when adding], 'If Allah wills.'" ARE BETTER THINGS COMING? INSHALLAH (*The New York Times*. January 25, 2022).

- *Simile*: it is a figure of speech that explicitly compares two things through some connectives such as "like" and "as". Sometimes, this is eased through the use of verbs like "resemble". In the excerpt that follows, Ramadan has been likened to a marathon because it involves a sense of solidarity and self-struggle that Muslim people observe and since it is the month when charity work and philanthropy in the Muslim community increase:

> 'Ramadan is like a marathon,' said Mr. Ocasio We start the month with no way to pay for all of this, but the community always comes

together to sponsor us so we can go out and feed the people.' WHY RAMADAN GENERATES MILLIONS IN CHARITABLE GIVING EVERY YEAR (*The New York Times*. April 29, 2022).

- *Anaphora*: it consists of repeating a sequence of words, thereby lending emphasis at the beginnings of neighbouring clauses. Halliday and Hasan (1976) have noted that in longer turns, or texts in general, repetition can also have a cohesive function "since it can stabilize both reference and topic across a stretch of discourse." The writer of the next extract has repeated the clause "I worry about" five times in different places to emphasize that he is having pathos for Muslims and is very concerned with the problems they endure either in their homelands or other locations:

> *I worry about* Muslims. Islam teaches me to care about all human beings, and animals too, but life is short and I can't even find enough time to worry about all the Muslims ... *I do worry about* the Muslims who face extinction at the hands of other Muslims in their own homelands ... But mostly *I worry about* my kind of Muslims, those who are expected to explain to the world what real Islam is like ... *I worry about* the pundits who end up on TV within hours of an atrocity and are required to condemn or defend and explain on our behalf. *I worry about* those nice folk who are supposed to remind the world that Islam is a religion of peace. I WORRY ABOUT MUSLIMS (*The New York Times*. December 17, 2015).

- *Neologism*: this refers to newly coined terms, words, or phrases that may be in the process of entering common use, yet they have not been accepted in mainstream language. In extract [S3], the writer has coined the term "letterism" (in Arabic *Hurufiyya*), an aesthetic movement that appeared amongst artists from Muslim countries in the second half of the twentieth century. These artists have dwelt on their comprehension of traditional Islamic calligraphy in their conception of modern art. It has been claimed that neologism, as well as linguistic experimentation is an important part of the American spirit (Jasinski, 2001), which tends to borrow and domesticate certain linguistic codes – always not English – for both communicative and persuasive usage:

> One of the pioneers of the movement that came to be known as *Hurufiyya* (or *"letterism"*, Ms. Umar, who died at age 97 in 2005, started experimenting with Arabic letters in the 1940s, integrating calligraphy into modern art. In this work, she used the Arabic letter

"ein" to create an abstract nocturnal landscape. STARTING NEW CONVERSATIONS ABOUT ARAB ART (*The New York Times*. October 3, 2023. S3).

- *Euphemism*: it is the substitution of one more pleasant expression for one whose meaning may come across as rude or offensive. The headline of extract [A21] includes the expression "ethnic cleansing" which was opted for in the place of "genocide." These terms are the same, but one is stronger, and the other is not. Another euphemism is "a rotting of the flower" that is symptomatic of decline and corruption. Whenever readers encounter euphemisms in texts, they ought to reflect upon their presence as powerful sensations (e.g. embarrassment, fear, disgust, and so on) remain out of sight. Most frequently, this device produces a rhetorical effect because it masks and obfuscates meaning:

    It is the ugly side of Myanmar's democratic transition — *a rotting of the flower*, even as it seems to bloom. ETHNIC CLEANSING IN MYANMAR (*The New York Times*. July 13, 2012. A21).

- *Apostrophe*: it is a sudden turn from the general audience to address a specific group or a certain people, either absent or present, real or imagined. The second person pronoun "you" is remarkably very obscure because it is not clear who it refers to, nor whether it is intended to be interpreted as second person (i.e. the reader and a particular addressee) or as the equivalent of "one" (generic third person), which may, in turn, be interpreted as "I." (Jeffries & McIntyre, 2010) Consider the extract below that features in [A21]:

    Something can be said of America in the 1950s. But over the ensuing decades, the Protestant establishment crumbled and America became more marvelously diverse. If you're reading this, there is a good chance you're a member of a minority group – or several. Maybe you're Black or Jewish or Muslim. THE AGE OF THE CREATIVE MINORITY (*The New York Times*. November 24, 2021. A21).

- *Synecdoche*: it is closely linked to metonymy and sometimes it is considered as a subclass of it. Originally, it means accepting a part as responsible for the whole or vice-versa. In extract [SR11], the writer has used the term "the capital" as one lexical item to refer back to England and/or its government:

> One of the more surprising aspects of Elisabethan England is that its foreign and economic policy was driven by a close alliance with the Islamic world, a fact conveniently ignored today by those pushing the populist rhetoric of national sovereignty… <u>The capital</u> was used to fund the costs of commercial voyages, and the profits – or losses – would also be shared. ENGLAND'S FORGOTTEN MUSLIM HISTORY (*The New York Times*. September 17, 2016. SR11).

- *Metonymy*: it is another rhetorical trope used in the discourse of the NYT, in which a concept or a thing is not called by its own name but by the name of something intimately linked to that concept. As a conceptual phenomenon, metonymy first caught the attention of cognitive linguists in 1980, the publication date of George Lakoff and Mark Johnson's influential book *Metaphors We Live By*, in which the linguistic function of metonymy is claimed to be mainly one of indirect reference (e.g. the crown standing for 'the monarchy'), i.e. as a relationship where one entity "stands for" another. (Panther & Thornburg, 2003) In the following extract, for instance, the name "Ibrahim" is used as a metonym for a hopeful prayer and a close friendship with God. More significantly, this particular name represents monotheism:

> So, we named our son "*Ibrahim.*" One might assume it's because "*Ibrahim,*" the Arabic pronunciation of Abraham, is the dear friend of God revered by all monotheistic religions, who rebuilt the Ka'ba in Mecca, offered to sacrifice his son, and was promised a blessed progeny that would inherit the land … The name is in fact a hopeful prayer -- both for my son and the future of America. It's inspired by a verse in the Quran: "O fire, be coolness and peace upon *Ibrahim.*" FOR MUSLIM-AMERICANS, BABY AIDAN OR BABY MUHAMMAD? (*The New York Times*. October 3, 2015).

- *Rhetorical Question*: it is one form of a question that is raised in order to make a point. The question is used as a rhetorical device in order to incite the reader to consider the message in its totality. In the extract that follows, the writer raised two rhetorical questions: one in the headline and the other in the opening paragraph (the lead). The intent is to provoke the readers, engage them and underscore the importance of Arabic numerals:

> Should Americans, as part of their school curriculum, learn Arabic numerals? CivicScience, a Pittsburgh-based research firm, put that question to some 3,200 Americans recently in a poll seemingly about mathematics, but the outcome was a measure of students' attitudes

toward the Arab world. Some 56 percent of the respondents said, "No." Fifteen percent had no opinion. WHO'S AFRAID OF ARABIC NUMERALS? (*The New York Times.* June 4, 2019).

- *Antithesis*: it includes the rhetorical contrast of ideas through the juxtaposition of words, clauses or sentences. Most of the time, these ideas include compound sentences (two independent clauses), which are separated by a comma or a semicolon. In certain occasions, the antithesis may feature as a compound sentence with a conjunction. The next excerpt is illustrative of this device since the news reporter states that Muslims have lived in the United States of America for many centuries; however, they have been unlucky to pen their own narrative. Because of this, they were frequently ridiculed and screened as the foreign or the "Other":

> If you aren't writing your story, others will write it for you. That's what happened to Muslims in America for too long. <u>We've been in this country since the sixteenth century</u>, but <u>we've rarely had the opportunity to tell our own stories in history books, movies and television shows</u>. Instead we have been cast as America's villains, foreigners and invaders. I WISH I'D HAD 'RAMY' WHEN I WAS A KID (*The New York Times.* June 9, 2020).

- *Parallelism*: it refers to the balance achieved between one or more sentences of similar phrases or clauses having the same grammatical structure. In the next excerpt, the reporter has established a parallel construction between different phrases: "the scarf of a Muslim woman"; "the skullcap of an observant Jew"; "the turban of a Sikh" through the coordinating conjunction 'and', which is usually employed to tie all these noun phrases and hence produce a rhetorical and tuneful effect (for more details, see Chapter 8) -- such parallel patterns are pleasurable to the human inner ears:

> The laws, their rationale and their enforcement differ from country to country, even school to school. But the fact is that any such regulation is inherently discriminatory because the targets are likely to be members of faiths that mandate outward signs. *The scarf of a Muslim woman, the skullcap of an observant Jew* and *the turban of a Sikh* cannot be concealed. MUSLIMS IN EUROPEAN SCHOOLS (*The New York Times.* October 8, 2003).

- *Borrowings*: they are loanwords borrowed from a donor language and incorporated into a recipient language. The writer of the excerpt [A19] has dwelt on a borrowing (i.e. Irmee wara dahrak) to problematize unwanted behaviour, such as bullying, that some Muslim women frequently experience due to the wearing of the Hijab. Certainly, the NYT writers' tendency to use borrowings signify that they are well-informed about Muslim cultures, countries and communities:

   One time, I came home so exhausted I couldn't even make it up to my room. I slumped at the bottom of the stairs; my mom sat next to me. She didn't ask what was wrong. Instead, she shared stories of her own experiences. Like when her colleagues looked askance at her when she began wearing her hijab at work. In the customary Egyptian folk wisdom, she said, in Arabic, "Irmee wara dahrak," translated, "Throw it behind your back." She also pointed out that bullying happens to many people for many reasons. A MUSLIM CHRISTMAS STORY (*The New York Times*. December 23, 2018. A19).

- *Allegory*: it is a rhetorical device wherein characters or events in a particular discourse represent, illustrate or symbolize certain complex ideas and concepts in ways that are both tangible and digestible. Extract [A21] illustrates this metaphorical side of language, in which the writer has used the bottle of cologne Bashar al-Assad once saw in his father's office as one allegory for Syria. The bottle might be the same, yet Syria is not. Similar to a metaphor, allegory is employed in the NYT discourse for rhetorical ornamentation. Very often, it articulates a relationship, one of similarity, between what the words affirm and another, intended meaning (Wright, 2009):

   The president "remembers seeing a big bottle of cologne on a cabinet next to his father's desk," Mr. Belt wrote. "He was amazed to find it still there 27 years later, practically untouched." *The bottle can be seen as an allegory for Syria itself.* MY SYRIA, AWAKE AGAIN AFTER 40 YEARS (The *New York Times*. June 27, 2011. A21).

- *Honorifics*: these are titles or expressions with connotations conveying respect, politeness and esteem. They are used particularly when referring to people. Allan (2009) assumes that the commonest form of referent honorifics are honorary titles used in conjunction with a name. Many languages have honorary titles; the English form *Mr* and the German form *Herr* derive from nouns designating higher social roles or divine beings. Also common are titles deriving from the names of kin terms or of occupation that are considered high in social standing (e.g., uncle, aunt, doctor, professor) or from ranks in specific social groups, such as military units (general) and business groups. The extract below that revolves around the annual celebration of Eid al-Fitr and the outfits Muslims wear on this occasion at Washington Square Park and New York City, involves some referent honorifics, namely the term "Imam" (i.e. a title reserved for a prayer leader in a mosque within the Islamic tradition) and "Mr." which is often placed before the names of males, whether they are married or not, to show respect:

> "We were just trying to conceptualize space that could fit our growing numbers and be a memorable experience," said the center's director, <u>Imam</u> Khalid Latif, who led this year's prayer before giving a khutbah, or sermon "It can be very affirming knowing that in a city as large as New York, you're not by yourself, you're not alone," <u>Mr.</u> Khalid added. "And it helps people also around us who we share space with, who are our neighbors, to know that we're Muslim, and we are here as well." GETTING DRESSED FOR THE 'MUSLIM MET GALA' (*The New York Times.* April 10, 2024. ST4).

- *The Editorial "We"*: it is used in newspapers and other print media forms by columnists and commentators. The editorial "We" refers to journalists while expressing their opinions about certain issues and topics as one way of involving readers, manipulating their minds and directing their opinions. In the next extract, for instance, the reporter has used this rhetorical device to add dignity to his story when he suggested that conflict is avoidable between the West and the rest – Islamic, Hindu, Japanese, etc., if civilizations collaborate with one another and countries relinquish blind interests:

> Cultures evolve. Recent decades have seen democratic values take hold in Portugal, Spain, Japan, Taiwan and other countries far from the Protestant individualism that Mr. Huntington sees as the bedrock of Western ways. <u>We</u> need not and should not assume an inexorable conflict between "the West and the rest". "<u>We</u> should turn a potential for conflict into a practice of mutual gain. INTERESTS CLASH BUT CIVILIZATIONS CAN COOPERATE (*The New York Times.* January 7, 1997).

- *Maxims*: they are simple and concrete sayings, popularly known and repeated by people. They express a general truth based on common sense or the practical experience of human beings. In extract [SR1], the writer started off using one maxim "In war, it's said, truth dies first", to naturalize the claim that truth is the first thing to be lost in wars. As a matter of truth, maxims are used as one stylistic trope that carries the weight of popular wisdom, and they can help in both argumentation and persuasion:

> *In war, it's said, truth dies first.* LIFE DURING WARTIME (*The New York Times.* July 22, 2012. SR1).

- *Embedding*: it is the process by which one clause is included (embedded) in another. More broadly, embedding refers to the inclusion of any linguistic unit as part of another unit of the same general type. In the next excerpt, the writer has resolved to include three secondary clauses (e.g. that inspired the Quakers; who served as a minister in the court of an Almohad caliph; which became the main source for European rediscovery of the Greeks) within the main clauses with the objective of developing his ideas and expanding the meaning potential. The relative pronouns such as "that", "who", and "which" have created embedding relations between clauses in the extract below:

> The insights in Ibn Tufayl's work that inspired the Quakers also shined in the works of Abul-Walid Muhammad Ibn Rushd, also known as Averroes. Ibn Tufayl, who served as a minister in the court of an Almohad caliph of Islamic Spain, commissioned Ibn Rushd to write commentaries on ancient Greek philosophy, which became the main source for European rediscovery of the Greeks, earning him great reverence in Western intellectual history. THE MUSLIMS WHO INSPIRED SPINOZA, LOCKE AND DEFOE (*The New York Times*, April 5, 2021).

- *Allusion*: it is a rhetorical trope that communicates versatile meanings in a few words by pointing in an implicit way to a well-known event, person or place. When the NYT writers draw on allusions, they assume that they share a "body of common knowledge with their audience, and this audience will be able to recognize their reference." (Sorensen, 2012, p. 18) In the next excerpt, the writer has alluded to "The Roots of the Muslim Rage", a famous essay that was drafted in 1990 by the Middle Eastern scholar and British American historian, Bernard Lewis, who specialized in Oriental Studies.

> U.S. policies are often blamed for *Muslim rage.* AMERICA NEEDS TO LISTEN TO MUSLIMS (*The New York Times.* February 28, 2003).

- *Epistemic Modality*: it is one type of linguistic modality dealing with a speaker / writer's judgment or evaluation, which is the degree of confidence or belief of the knowledge upon which the proposition is grounded. In other words, epistemic modality has mainly to do with the way speakers / writers communicate their doubts, certainties, and guesses about certain debatable issues. In the extract that follows, the NYT reporter addresses Pope Francis' advocacy for more intense dialogue with world religions, and he hinges upon two different language functions, namely advice and possibility. The latter functions are conveyed through these dissimilar modal verbs: 'should" and "can", both of which designate actions happening in the future. Endley (2010, p. 273) notes that "epistemic modality involves the speaker's knowledge or belief concerning some situation that has occurred, is occurring, or will occur":

> Francis of Assisi, the Pope said, also "tells us we should work to build peace," which can come about only by overcoming a relativistic view of the world ... "My wish is that the dialogue between us should help to build bridges connecting all people, in such a way that everyone can see in the other not an enemy, not a rival, but a brother or sister to be welcomed and embraced," he said. POPE APPEALS FOR MORE INTERRELIGIOUS DIALOGUE (*The New York Times*. March 22, 2013).

Obviously, the variety of the above rhetorical tropes reveals that the NYT discourse is very rich (somewhat biased like all media), complex and even spectacular, when it comes to its style and rhetoric. Such richness is natural because of the calibre and professionalism of its reporters in the domain of journalism and elite press, who are, and to borrow Facchinetti et al. (2012, p. 145), "the gatekeepers of information, the filters of facts, the safeguards of truth, the manipulative eye, the interpretive voice." Their style remains distinctive and a fertile ground where stylisticians, rhetoricians and discourse analysts can not only explore the mesmerizing and very impactful aspects of language, but also how this particular language works on certain people and changes their thoughts and even their actions.

11.8 Conclusion

This chapter has found out that the writers of the NYT cannot go without making selections at the level of stylistic and rhetorical uses of language because these selections allow them to construct and build up strong arguments about other people and cultures. In addition to the form, which is seemingly designed to differentiate the NYT discourse from other forms of writing, the content of opinion pieces and news stories is selected following the highest standards to attract a large public. It may be true to say that language provides people with different choices, but the NYT's style provides readers with a highly informative and persuasive style that does combine between ingenuity and sometimes subjectivity.

11.9 Further Readings

Bogart, L. (1989). *Press and public: Who reads what, when, where, and why in American newspapers.* Hillsdale, NJ: Lawrence Erlbaum Associates, Inc.

Frost, C. (2012). *Designing for newspapers and magazines.* New York: Routledge.

Harris, R. A. (2017). *Writing with clarity and style: A guide to rhetorical devices for contemporary writers.* New York: Routledge.

McGuigan, B. (2007). *Rhetorical devices: A handbook and activities for student writers.* Clayton, DE: Prestwick House, Inc.

Richardson, J. (2013). *Language and journalism.* London: Taylor & Francis.

11.10 Questions for Discussion

1) Which functions does language play?
2) Are there any other functions you came across in the previous chapters?
3) In your view, why do the NYT reporters draw on rhetorical devices?
4) How can you describe the style of the NYT discourse?
5) Do you agree that style is a motivated option?

General Conclusion

Style, Meaning and Pedagogy has aimed to provide undergraduate students and teacher practitioners with some useful instruments that they can adopt in their critical reading and examination of literary and non-literary texts. Here, I must insist, as Hardy (1973, p. 26) did before me, that "what we give our students in the universities is indeed the fruits of our scholarship", which we develop and enrich continually thanks to our interactions with research and teaching environments.

Part I has detailed the complexity of style in literary texts in different types of poetry. In the first chapter, key definitions of style and poetry have been juxtaposed to stress their shifty and dynamic aspects, a fact which presupposes prior knowledge about the trends that marked the histories of each concept. That is, a good grasp of poetry and style remains contingent upon a good understanding of their intellectual movements and schools of thought. The second chapter was practice-based since it encompassed the semantic and pragmatic meanings of the narrative poem, "Abou Ben Adhem" which was penned by the British poet Leigh Hunt. The critical analysis covered metaphorical expressions, lexical and syntactic structures and other aesthetic dimensions that helped the poem stand out amidst other genres of poetry. Indeed, what was so stunning about this poem was both its ability to pigeonhole dreams as divine gifts and its resolution to screen two meanings of love: horizontal and vertical.

As metaphors were integral to poetry and they served both to embellish and obscure its text, the third chapter was consecrated to E.B. Browning's poem, "How Do I Love Thee? Let Me Count The Ways." It was found that metaphors were not coincidental, especially in love poetry, for they were so capable of connecting the speaker to the addressee, who had to respond more positively to them. Put differently, conceptual metaphors were amenable to creating friendship, bridging simultaneously the gap between human beings and forging emotional and intellectual ties among lovers.

Then, the fourth chapter has put into practice Halliday's theory of transitivity and implemented it in E. Bishop's poem, "Manners." The stylistic approach suggested was not only retrievable and verifiable, but it was exhaustive as it moved from the superficial to the pragmatic level of the text. The salient outcomes of this chapter were twofold: the cooperative principle was intrinsic to human relationships, and manners were not a matter of words (i.e. verbal processes), but they were rather a matter of actions and deeds (i.e. physical processes).

The fifth chapter presented an innovative way of approaching short poems, as is the case with "Memory", by exposing the readers to a flexible method of analysis (i.e. aberrant decoding), so they can study efficiently abstract concepts such as face and beauty and better discern their multiple guises. My great concern was to prove that the reading of poetry necessitates attentive as well as resistant reading that does not necessarily align with the imposed / intentional reading of the speaker / poet. My detailed analysis yielded the following results: 1) short poems could be analyzed line by line; and 2) aberrant reading could challenge dominant meanings and offer an alternative voice to them.

While probing into other types of metaphors, the sixth chapter, which addressed goal- setting and dialogism, has cast some light on Afro-American dreams and goals; it took advantage of the constructivist approach to investigate worthwhile issues like equity and racial equality that never cease to provoke the masses since the Harlem Renaissance. Among the findings of this chapter was that some texts could be better understood when they are projected against or read in the light of others. In other words, if readers wanted to fully fathom Hughes' poem "Dreams", it is recommended that they revisit Martin Luther King's rhetorical speech, "I Have a Dream." The seventh chapter traced up the genesis of reader-response theory and its pertinence to the study of meaning and style. It resorted to a motivational poem, "Thinking" -- not dissimilar to Hughes' "Dreams" -- and it fronted students' creative responses, which oscillated between appreciation and enjoyment. The outcome of this in-classroom experience was the premise that motivational poetry and the creative responses to it resulted in boosting students' diligence and assiduity. Meanwhile, they altered their negative attitudes towards poetry and its perplexing style.

In the eighth chapter, O'Meara's pandemic poem, "And the People Stayed Home", was called for to delineate the new home of the recent shutdown and pinpoint the therapeutic potentials of poetry and its numerous healing powers. I remarked that the pandemic home was an exceptional home because it gratified human beings' hierarchy needs. This home, which substituted the public space, had provided people with different possibilities to practice all their activities wavering between work and leisure. Besides, I have found that pandemic poetry leaned more towards prose and thrived more in the digital space.

The ninth chapter described a popular painting by Laurentius de Voltolina; moreover, it revisited the theory of learning styles and lecture-based instruction in the medieval age. This respective chapter sought to scrutinize the notion of style and its inherent relevance to and connection with methodologies of teaching and learning. The semiotic analysis of the painting, dwelling on MDA, had foregrounded other aspects of classroom discourse, which might furbish readers' skills in terms of visual signs' interpretations. The most resonant finding of this chapter was that lecture-based instruction was a double-edged sword, as it lacked interactiveness and did not foster the full engagement of students, who appeared to exhibit divergent behaviours in the classroom sphere.

Part two was devoted to the study of non-literary texts like blurbs, headlines and news stories / opinion pieces; the tenth chapter mulled over students' critical essays on the style of headlines and blurbs, and it suggested some helpful ways and guidelines for examining such genres of texts more efficiently. This chapter was useful not because it drew analogies between students' stylistic reflections, but mainly because it offered the students themselves a chance to articulate their apprehensions of style and meaning when it comes to blurbs and headlines. Also, the approach initiated here was not top-down but rather a bottom-up approach to media texts.

Last but not least, the eleventh chapter debated the old question of the newspaper's prime purpose: Is it informing or persuading? By giving the example of the NYT and delving into its news stories and opinion pieces, the chapter stressed the idea of choice and selection that appertained to the media discourse. Several rhetorical devices have been clustered and fully discussed to guide the readers to be more conscious of the phenomenon of subjectivity and bias in discourse. This rhetorical analysis, aside from proving to be a highly relevant methodological tool to the study of meaning and style, was geared towards enhancing the critical thinking skills of EFL learners, and encouraging researchers, in Applied / Literary Linguistics and beyond, to further experiment with the aesthetics and poetics of human language.

My hope is that all the chapters above will present a wealth of information on the key questions within the area of classroom discourse, ignite the reader's passion for style, and benefit them in their academic career through the enhancement of their comprehension, analytical and synthetic skills so that they can not only enjoy but also decorticate and judge meaning duly and properly across multiple text genres.

List of References

Abercrombie, N., & Longhurst, B. (2007). *The Penguin dictionary of media studies*. London: Clays Ltd.

Acim, R. (2021). Why narrative poetry still matters in stylistics. *Journal of educational research and practice*, 11, pp. 439 - 453, https://doi.org/10.5590/JERAP.2021.11.1.31

Adams, J., & Neal, C. S. (2018). *How do I love thee?* New York: HarperCollins.

Adams, J. T. (1931). *The epic of America*. New York: Triangle Books.

Afuape, T. (2011). *Power, resistance and liberation in therapy with survivors of trauma: To have our hearts broken*. New York: Routledge.

Aggarwal, J. C. (2001). *Principles, methods and techniques of teaching*. New Delhi: Vikas Publishing House.

Airey, D., & Tribe, J. (2005). *An international handbook of tourism education*. New York: Routledge.

Akyol, M. (2021). The Muslims that inspired Spinoza, Locke and Defoe. *The New York Times*, https://www.nytimes.com/2021/04/05/opinion/enlightenment-islam-robinson-crusoe.html

-----------. (2019). Who's afraid of Arabic numerals? *The New York Times*, https://www.nytimes.com/2019/06/04/opinion/arabic-numerals.html

Alexander, P. A., & Winne, P. H. (2012). *Handbook of educational psychology*. London: Routledge.

Ali, W. (2015). For Muslim-Americans: Baby Aidan or baby Muhammad. *The New York Times*, https://www.nytimes.com/2015/10/04/opinion/sunday/for-muslim-americans-baby-aidan-or-baby-muhammad.html

--------. (2020). I wish I'd had 'Ramy' when I was a kid. *The New York Times*, https://www.nytimes.com/2020/06/09/opinion/ramy-Youssef-muslim-representation.html

Alford, H. (2017). New neighbors, new considerations. *The New York Times*, https://www.nytimes.com/2017/10/04/style/refugee-dinners.html

Allan, K. (2009). *Concise encyclopedia of semantics*. Burlington: Elsevier Ltd.

Alvarez, A. (1988). Martin Luther King's "I have a dream": The speech event as metaphor. *Journal of black studies*, 18 (3), pp. 337-357, DOI:10.1177/002193478801800306

Anderson, L. (2007). *Beauty and truth: Plato's greater Hippias and Aristotle's poetics*. Millis, MA: Agora Publications.

Annison, J. E. (2000). Towards a clearer understanding of the meaning of "home." *Journal of intellectual & developmental disability*, 25 (4), pp. 251-262. https://doi.org/10.1080/13668250020019566-1

Applegate, E. (2005). *Strategic copywriting: How to create effective advertising*. Lanham, Md: Rowman & Littlefield.

Aridi, S. (2021). How the pandemic has transformed the idea of home. *The New York Times*, https://www.nytimes.com/2021/03/13/at-home/pandemic-home.html

Atassi, M. A. (2011). My Syria, awake again after 40 years. *The New York Times*. http://www.nytimes.com/2011/06/27/opinion/27Atassi.html

Atkinson, B. (1940). *The complete essays and other writings of Ralph Waldo Emerson*. New York: Random House.

Aubrey, K., & Riley, A. (2022). *Understanding and using educational theories*. London: Sage Publications Ltd.

Austin, M. (2015). *Reading the world: Ideas that matter.* New York: Norton & Company, Inc.

Azuike, M. N. (1992). Style: Theories and practical application. *Language sciences*, 14 (1/2), pp. 109-127, https://doi.org/10.1016/0388-0001(92)90016-8

Baker, P., & Ellece, S. (2011). *Key terms in discourse analysis*. London: Continuum International Publishing Group.

Bakhtin, M. M. (1984). *Problems of Dostoevsky's poetics* (Trans. C. Emerson). Minneapolis: U of Minnesota Press.

Barkley, E., & Major, C. H. (2018). *Interactive lecturing: A Handbook for college faculty*. San Francisco, CA: Jossey-Bass.

Barthes, R. (1967). *Elements of semiology*. London: Cape.

Bawer, B. (2003). Arranged marriages prevent integration: A trap for Muslim women in Europe. *The New York Times*, https://www.nytimes.com/2003/06/27/opinion/IHT-arranged-marriages-prevent-integration-a-trap-for-muslim-women-in.html

Belcher, D. (2023). Starting new conversations about Arab art. *The New York Times*. https://www.nytimes.com/2023/10/03/arts/museum-modern-arab-art-qatar.html

Bell, A., Ensslin, A., van der Bom, I., & Smith, J. (2019). A reader response method not just for 'you.' *Language and literature*, 28 (3), pp. 241-262. https://doi.org/10.1177/0963947019859954

Bennett, A. (1999). *Romantic poets and the culture of posterity*. Cambridge, UK: Cambridge U Press.

Benson, A. C. (2019). *Escape and other essays*. Frankfurt am Main: Outlook Verlag GmbH.

Bishop, J. (2021). *Cases on technologies in education from classroom 2.0 to society 5.0*. Hershey, Pennsylvania: IGI Global.

Black, E. (2006). *Pragmatic stylistics*. Edinburgh: Edinburgh U Press Ltd.

Bleakney, E. (2009). *Poem in your pocket*. New York: Harry N. Abrams, Inc.

Bonyadi, A. (2019). Discourse analysis and language pedagogy: A review. *Journal of teacher education for sustainability*, 21 (1), pp. 128-136, DOI: https://doi.org/10.2478/jtes-2019-0010

Boorstein, M. (2020). A quarter of Americans, and a majority of black Protestants, say their religious faith has deepened because of coronavirus. *The Washington Post*, https://www.washingtonpost.com/religion/2020/04/30/coronavirus-deepening-more-religious-black-protestants/

Boufford, D. (1998). *Adjectives and adverbs: Essential English skills*. Dayton, OH: Milliken Publishing Company.

Bradford, R. (1997). *Stylistics*. London: Routledge.

Branston, G., & Stafford, R. (2010). *The media student's book*. London: Routledge.

Brooks, D. (2007). A new global blueprint. *The New York Times*, https://www.nytimes.com/2007/06/19/opinion/19brooks.html

---------------. (2021). The age of the creative minority. *The New York Times*, https://www.nytimes.com/2021/11/24/opinion/creative-minority-multiculturalism.html

Brotton, J. (2016). England's forgotten Muslim history. *The New York Times*, https://www.nytimes.com/2016/09/18/opinion/sunday/englands-forgotten-muslim-history.html

Brown, B. S. (2013). *Realizing dreams from A-Z: Principles for excellence*. Bloomington, IN: AuthorHouse.

Brown, G., & Yule, G. (1983). *Discourse analysis*. Cambridge: Cambridge U. Press.

Brown, J. K. (2007). Theoretical perspectives on Scripture as communication. *Scripture as communication: Introducing Biblical hermeneutics* (pp. 19-120). Michigan: Baker Academic.

Brown, P., & Levinson, S. C. (1987). *Politeness: Some universals in language usage*. Cambridge: Cambridge U Press.

Brundrett, M., & Rhodes, C. (2014). *Researching educational leadership and management: Methods and approaches*. London: Sage.

Buckenmeyer, R. (2009). *Philosophy of Maria Montessori: What it means to be human*. Bloomington, IN: Xlibris Corporation.

Burke, M. (2014). *The Routledge handbook of stylistics*. London and New York: Routledge.

Cameron, L. (2003). *Metaphor in educational discourse*. London: Continuum.

Campbell, L. (1883). *The Theaetetus of Plato*. London: Henry Frowde.

Carroll, R. (2005). Finding the words to say it: The healing power of poetry. *eCAM*, 2 (2), 161-172, doi:10.1093/ecam/neh096

Clark, S., & Pointon, G. (2016). *The Routledge student guide to English usage: A guide to academic writing for students*. London: Routledge.

Clemens, W. C. (1997). Interests clash but civilizations can cooperate. *The New York Times*, https://www.nytimes.com/1997/01/07/opinion/IHT-interests-clash-but-civilizations-can-cooperate.html

Cluysenaar, A. (1976). *Introduction to literary stylistics*. London: Batsford.

Constantine, L. (2012). *Modern poetry*. Indiana: Xlibris Corporation.

Cottrell, E. (2007). *The medical student's survival guide: The early years*. Oxford: Radcliffe Publishing Ltd.

Cox, P. L., & Parker, B. K. (2013). *Exploring heavenly places – Travel guide to the width, length, depth and height* (vol. 9). Apple Valley, CA: Aslan's Place Publications.

Crouch, D., & Rutherford, J. (2014). Reading and reception. In: A. Elliott, (ed.), *Routledge handbook of social and cultural theory* (pp. 358-373). London: Routledge.

Cuddon, J. A. (1998). *The Penguin dictionary of literary terms and literary theory*. London: Penguin Books.

----------------. (2013). *A dictionary of literary terms and literary theory*. Chester, West Sussex: Wiley-Blackwell.

Cull, N. J., Holbrook, D., & Welch, D. (2003). *Propaganda and mass persuasion: A historical encyclopedia, 1500 to the present*. Santa Barbara, California: ABC-CLIO.

Davis, T. F., & Womack, K. (2002). *Formalist criticism and reader-response theory* (pp. 11- 90). New York: Palgrave.

Deleuze, G., & Guattari, F. (1983). What is a minor literature? (Trans. B. Robert). *Mississipi Review*, 11 (3), pp. 13-33.

Denham, K., & Lobeck, A. (2013). *Linguistics for everyone: An introduction*. Boston, MA: Wadsworth.

Desmond, K. K. (2011). *Ideas about art*. Chester, West Sussex: Wiley-Blackwell.

Diffey, T. J. (2016). The roots of imagination: The philosophical context. In: S. Prickett (ed.), *The Romantics* (pp. 164-201). New York: Routledge

Doiron, M. (2013). *Thread of life: An adoption story*. Bloomington, IN: iUniverse.

Dong, A. (2006). *The language of design: Theory and computation*. London: Springer-Verlag.

Duiker, W. J., & Spielvogel, J. J. (2016). *World history* (vol. I: To 1800). Boston, MA: Cengage Learning.

Duke, R. K. (1990). *The persuasive appeal of the chronicler: A rhetorical analysis*. New York: Sheffield Academic Press.

Durant, W. (2022). Aristotle and Greek science. *The story of philosophy* (pp. 46-84). New York: Dover Publications.

Easthope, H. (2010). A place called home. *Housing, theory and society*, 21 (3), pp. 128-138, https://doi.org/10.1080/14036090410021360

Echaore-McDavid, S. (2006). *Career opportunities in education and related services*. New York: Ferguson.

Eco, U. (1972). Towards a semiotic inquiry into the television message. *Working papers in cultural studies*, no. 6, C.C.C.S., U of Birmingham.

Eisner, E. (2009). The Lownfeld lecture 2008: What education can learn from the arts. *Art education*, 62 (2), pp. 6-9, DOI:10.1080/00043125.2009.11519006

Eldik, Y. (2018). A Muslim Christmas story. *The New York Times*, https://www.nytimes.com/2018/12/23/opinion/muslim-christmas.html

Eliot, T. S. (2010). *The waste land and other poems*. Canada: Broadview Press.

Emerson, R. W. (1898). *Nature, addresses, and lectures*. Boston: Houghton, Mifflin and Company.

Endley, M. J. (2010). *Linguistic perspectives on English grammar: A guide for EFL teachers*. Charlotte, NC: Information Age Publishing Inc.

England, K. (2014). Producing feminist geographies: Theory, methodologies and research strategies. In: S. C. Aitken., & G. Valentine (eds.), *Approaches to human geography* (pp. 361-372). Los Angeles: Sage.

Engle, J. (2021). What do you think are the secrets to happiness? *The New York Times*, https://www.nytimes.com/2021/03/19/learning/what-do-you-think-are-the-secrets-to- happiness.html

Entwistle, N., & Tait, H. (1990). Approaches to learning, evaluations of teaching, and preferences for contrasting academic environments. *Higher education*, 19, pp. 169-194, DOI: https //doi.org/10.1007/BF00137106

Etnier, L. J. (2009). *Bring your "A" game: A young athlete's guide to mental toughness*. Chapell Hill: U of North Carolina Press.

Facchinetti, R., Brownlees, N , & Bös, B., Fries, U. (2012). *News as changing texts: Corpora, methodologies and analysis*. Cambridge: Cambridge Scholars.

Fairclough, A. (1995). *Martin Luther King, Jr*. London: U of Georgia Press.

Farndon, J. (2014). *So, you think you're clever?: Taking on the Oxford and Cambridge questions*. London: Icon Books Ltd.

Ferber, M. (2010). *Romanticism: A very short introduction*. New York: Oxford U Press Inc.

Flowerdew, J. (2013). *Discourse in English language instruction*. New York: Routledge.

Fowler, R. (1977). *Linguistics and the novel*. London: Methuen.

Francis, E. M. (2016). *Now that's a good question!: How to promote cognitive rigor through classroom questioning*. Alexandria, VA: ASCD.

Freud, S. (1900). The interpretations of dreams. In: J. Strachey (ed. and trans.). *The Standard edition of the complete psychological works of Sigmund Freud* (vols. 4-5). London: Hogarth Press.

Friedman, T. L. (2012). Getting to know you. *The New York Times*, http://www.nytimes.com/2012/01/15/opinion/sunday/friedman-getting-to-know-you.html

Fry, H., Ketteridge, S., & Marshall, S. (2003). *A handbook for teaching and learning in higher education: Enhancing academic practice*. London: Kogan.

Fyrenius, A., Bergdahl, E., & Silén, C. (2005). Lectures in problem-based learning -- why, when and how? An example of interactive lecturing that stimulates meaningful learning. *Medical teachers*, 27 (1), pp. 61-65, DOI:10.1080/01421590400016365

Gadd, T. R. (2006). *Classical poetry*. Ontario: S & S Materials.

Galtung, J. (1990). Cultural violence. *Journal of peace research*, 27 (3), pp. 291-305.

Gillsjö, C., & Schwartz-Barcott, D. (2011). A concept analysis of home and its meaning in the lives of three older adults." *Int j older people nurs*, 6 (1), pp. 4-12, https://doi.org/10.1111/j.1748-3743.2010.00207.x

Gönczöl-Davies, R. (2008). *Romanian: An essential grammar*. New York: Routledge.

Gonzales, P. (2012). *Red medicine: Traditional indigenous rites of birthing and healing*. Arizona: U of Arizona Press.

Gordon, D. R. (1998). *Philosophy and vision*. Amsterdam: Rodopi.

Granath, S. (2009). Who benefits from learning how to use corpora? In: K. Aijmer (ed.), *Corpora and language teaching* (pp. 47-66). The Netherlands: John Benjamin B.V.

Grice, P. (1989). Logic and conversation. In: H. P. Grice (ed.), *Studies in the ways of words* (pp. 22-40). Cambridge, MA: Harvard U Press.

Guerin, W. L., Labor, E., Morgan, L., Reesman, J. C., & Willingham, J. R. (2005). *Reader- response criticism. A handbook of critical approaches to literature* (pp. 350-377). New York: Oxford U Press.

Hall, S. (1973). *Encoding and decoding in the television discourse.* Birmingham: Center for Cultural Studies.

---------. (1997). *Representation: Cultural representations and signifying practices.* London: Sage.

Halliday, M. A. K. (2004). *Halliday's introduction to functional grammar.* New York: Routledge.

Halliday, M. A. K., & Hasan, R. (1976). *Cohesion in English.* London: Longman.

---------. (1985/1989). *Language, context, and text: Aspects of language in a social-semiotic perspective.* Oxford: Oxford U Press.

Halliday, M. A. K., & Matthiessen, C. (2006). *Construing experience through meaning: A language-based approach to cognition.* London: Bloomsbury Publishing.

Hamlyn, D. W. (2014). *Being a philosopher: The history of a practice.* London: Routledge.

Hanif, M. (2015). I worry about Muslims. *The New York Times*, https://www.nytimes.com/2015/12/18/opinion/i-worry-about-muslims.html

Hansen, V., & Curtis, K. R. (2017). *Voyages in world history.* Boston, MA: Cengage Learning.

Haqqani, H. (2003). America needs to listen to Muslims. *The New York Times*, https://www.nytimes.com/2003/02/28/opinion/IHT-popular-opinion-america-needs-to- listen-to-muslims.html

Hardy, B. (1973). The teaching of literature in the university: Some problems. *English in education,* 7 (1), pp. 26-38, DOI: 10.1111/j.1754-8845.1973.tb00403.x

Harrington, J. (2002). *Poetry and the public: The social form of modern U.S. poetics.* Middletown, Conn.: Wesleyan U Press.

Harris-Moore, D. (2014). *Media and the rhetoric of body perfection: Cosmetic surgery, weight, loss and beauty in popular culture.* London and New York: Routledge.

Hart, C. S. (2016). How do aspirations matter? *Journal of human development and capabilities,* 17 (3), pp. 324-341, DOI: 10.1080/19452829.2016.1199540

Hasan, S. (2024). Getting dressed for the 'Muslim met gala.' *The New York Times*, https://www.nytimes.com/2024/04/10/style/eid-ramadan-fashion-washington-square-park.html

Haser, V. (2005). *Metaphor, metonymy, and experientialist philosophy: Challenging cognitive semantics.* New York: Mouton de Gruyter.

Hasson, G. (2017). *Positive thinking: Find happiness and achieve your goals through the power of positive thought.* West Sussex: John Wiley & Sons Ltd.

Helin, J., Dahl, M., & de Monthoux, P. G. (2022). The power of daydreaming: The aesthetic act of a new beginning. *Culture and organization,* 28 (1), pp. 64- 78, DOI: 10.1080/14759551.2021.1986505

Herman, D., Jahn, M., & Ryan, M. (2005). *Routledge encyclopedia of narrative theory.* London: Routledge.

Hirsch, E. (1999). *How to read a poem and fall in love with poetry.* New York: Harcourt, Inc.

Hirvela, A. (2004). *Connecting reading & writing in second language writing instruction.* Ann Arbor, MI: U of Michigan Press.

Holdsworth, C., & Morgan, D. H. (2005). *Transitions in context: Leaving home, independence and adulthood.* New York: Open U Press.

Holloway, I., & Galvin, K. (2017). *Qualitative research in nursing and healthcare.* Chester, West Sussex: John Wiley & Sons, Ltd.

Høystad, O. M. (2007). *A history of the heart.* London: Reacktion Books Ltd.

Hughes, A. W. (2013). *Muslim identities: An introduction to Islam.* New York: Columbia U Press.

Hughes, G. (1989). *Words in time.* Oxford: Basil Blackwell.

Hughes, L. (1958). Harlem. *The Langston Hughes reader.* New York: George Braziller.

Ibrahim, Y. M. (1995). Europe's Muslim population: Frustrated, poor and divided. *The New York Times,* https://www.nytimes.com/1995/05/05/world/europe-s-muslim-population-frustrated-poor-and-divided.html

Ijpma, F. A., van de Graaf, R. C., Nicolai, J., & Meek, M. F (2006). The anatomy lesson of Dr. Nicolaes Tulp by Rembrandt (1632): A Comparison of the painting with a dissected left forearm of a Dutch male cadaver. *The journal of hand surgery,* 31 (6), pp. 882-891, DOI:10.1016/j.jhsa.2006.02.014

Iser, W. (1980). Interaction between text and reader. In: R. Suleiman., & I. Crosman, (eds.), *The reader in the text: Essays on audience and interpretation* (pp. 106-119). Princeton, NJ: Princeton U Press.

Janks, H., Locke, T. (2008). Discourse awareness in education: A critical perspective. In: Hornberger, N. H. (eds.), *Encyclopedia of language and education.* Boston MA: Springer, https://doi.org/10.1007/978-0-387-30424-3_137

Jarrad, J. C. (2012). *The case of the missing pronoun.* Bloomington, IN: Xlibris Corporation.

Jasinski, J. (2001). *Sourcebook on rhetoric: Key concepts in contemporary rhetorical studies.* Thousand Oaks, California: Sage Publications, Inc.

Jeffries, L., & McIntyre, D. (2010). *Stylistics.* Cambridge: Cambridge U Press.

Jesson-Dibley, D. (2003). *Leigh Hunt: Selected writings.* New York: Routledge.

Johnson, D. (2024). *The joy of children's literature* (3rd ed.). London: Routledge.

Johnson, M. (1981). *Philosophical perspectives on metaphor.* Minneapolis: U of Minnesota.

Jones, T. (2008). *A dreamer's diary: dethroning the underachiever.* Orlando FL: Xlibris Corporation.

Karlsson, N., Loewenstein, G., & McCafferty, J. (2004). The economics of meaning. *Nordic journal of political economy,* 30 (1), pp. 61-75.

Karolides, N. J. (2000). The transactional theory of literature. *Reader response theory in secondary and college classrooms* (pp. 3-24). Mahwah, NJ: Lawrence Erbaum Associates.

Kennedy, V. (2000). Metaphors in the news-introduction. *Metaphor and symbol,* 15 (4), pp. 209-211, DOI: 10.1207/S15327868MS1504_2

Kennedy, X. J. & Gioa, D. (1995). *Literature: Fiction, poetry, and drama.* New York: HarperCollings College Publishers.

Kern, R. (2000). *Literacy and language teaching.* New York: Oxford.

Kiwan, D. (2023). The contested scope of academic freedom. In: H. Tam, (ed.), *Who's afraid of political education?: The challenge to teach civic competence and democratic participation* (pp. 50-63). Bristol: Bristol U Press.

Kress, G., & van Leeuwen, T. (2002). Color as a semiotic mode: Notes for a grammar of color. *Visual communication,* 1 (3), pp. 343-368, DOI:10.1177/ 147035720200100306

-----------. (2006). *Reading images: The grammar of visual design.* London: Routledge.

Krug, N. (2020). The Story behind 'and the people stayed home,' the little poem that became so much more. *The Washington Post,* https://www.washingtonpost.com/entertainment/books/and-the-people-stayed-home-poem/2020/12/09/3f2411fe-3961-11eb-bc68-96af0daae728_story.html

Lakoff, G., & Johnson, M. (1980). Conceptual metaphor in everyday language. *The journal of philosophy,* 77 (8), pp. 453-486, https://doi.org/10.2307/2025464

Langdell, S. J. (2018). *Thomas Hoccleve: Religious reform, transnational poetics, and the invention of Chaucer.* Liverpool: Liverpool U Press.

Lawrenson, T. E., Sutcliffe, F. E., & Gadoffre, G. F. A. (1969). *Festschrift.* Manchester: Manchester U Press.

Leech, G., & Short, M. (2007). *Style in fiction: A linguistic introduction to English fictional prose.* Harlow, GA: Pearson.

Lewis, E. (2010). *Modernist image.* Newcastle upon Tyne: Cambridge Scholars Publishing.

Lewis, L. M. (2022). Elisabeth Barrett Browning: A poet's quest for ultimate reality, https://www.utpjournals.press/doi/pdf/10.3138/uram.28.1.4

Lieber, R. (2020). How to buy happiness (Responsibly). *The New York Times,* https://www.nytimes.com/2021/05/28/your-money/coronavirus-spending-happiness.html

Lim, K. (2000). *Practical guide to the I Ching.* Havelte, Holland: Binkey Kok Publications.

Lindsay, E. K. (1999). *An analysis of matches of teaching styles, learning styles and the uses of educational technology.* Unpublished Doctoral Dissertation, North Carolina State U, https://www.learntechlib.org/p/120623/

Linesenmeyer, M. (2021). Brief activities: Questioning, brainstorming, think-pair-share, jigsaw, and clinical case discussions. In: A. Fornari., & A. Poznanski (eds.), *How-to guide for active learning.* (pp. 39-66). Cham., Switzerland: Springer.

Lipsitz, G. (2006). *The possessive investment in whiteness: How people benefit from identity politics.* Philadelphia: Temple U Press.

Lock, S. (2014). *Mind: An emergent property.* Bloomington, Indiana: Xlibris LLC.

Lowe, W. (2011). Is the sun setting on lecture-based education? *International journal of therapeutic massage and bodywork,* 4 (4), pp. 7-9, DOI: 10.3822/ijtmb.v4i4.156

Lumpkin, S., & Seidensticker, J. (2011). *Rabbits: The animal answer guide*. Baltimore: John Hopkins U Press.

Mackey, J. (2009). *A practical and spiritual guide to personal healing: A mind, body, spirit approach*. Bloomington, IN: iUniverse, Inc.

Mackey, W. C. (1985). *Fathering behaviors: The dynamics of the man-child bond*. New York: Plenum Press.

Mahony, D. (2003). *Excel preliminary English*. Singapore: Green Giant Press.

Mallon, B. (2002). *Dream time with children: Learning to dream, dreaming to learn*. London: Jessica Kingsley Publishers.

Marte, J. (2016). Money can buy happiness – if you know how to use it. *The Washington Post*, https://www.washingtonpost.com/news/get-there/wp/2016/04/12/money-can-buy-happiness-if-you-know-how-to-use-it/

Martin, B., & Ringham, F. (2006). *Key terms in semiotics*. London: Continuum.

Martin, J. R. (2009). Discourse studies. In: M. A. K. Halliday., & J. J. Webster, (ed.), *Continuum companion to systemic functional linguistics* (pp. 154-165). London: Continuum International Publishing Group.

Martins, R. (2012). *Why dream but to make your dreams come true: How to find true happiness* (pp. 105-163). Bloomington, IN: Balboa.

Maslow, M. A. H. (1943). A theory of human motivation. *Psychological review*, 50 (4), pp. 370- 96, https://doi.org/10.1037/h0054346

Matoesian, G. M. (2001). *Law and the language of identity: Discourse in the William Kennedy Smith rape trial*. Oxford: Oxford U Press.

Maunder, A. (2010). *Encyclopedia of literary Romanticism*. New York: Facts On File, Inc.

Maybin, J., & Swann, J. (2010). *The Routledge companion to English language studies*. New York: Routledge.

McFarland, A. (2014). *Worldviews comparison*. Torrance, CA: Rose Publishing.

McIntosh, P., Lueck, R., & Davis, D. H. (2008). *Interpersonal communication skills in the workplace*. New York: American Management Association.

McIntosh, P., & Warren, D. (2013). *Creativity in the classroom: Case studies in using the arts in teaching and learning in higher education*. Bristol: Intellect Ltd.

McLuhan, H. M. (2013). The medium is the message. *Understanding media: The extensions of man*. Berkeley, California.

McQuillan, M. (1999). Reader-response theories. In: J. Wolfreys, (ed.), *Literary theories: A reader and guide* (pp. 139-148). New York, NY: New York U Press.

Merton, T., & Hart, P. (1985). *The literary essays of Thomas Merton*. New York: New Directions.

Mey, J. L. (2001). Context, implicature and reference. *Pragmatics: An introduction* (pp. 39- 56). Maldon, MA: Blackwell Publishing.

Meyer, M. (1996). *The compact Bedford introduction to literature*. Boston, MA: Stratford Publishing Services.

Mishra, R. C. (2005). *Teaching of information technology*. New Delhi: APH Publishing Corporation.

Moroni, S., & Lorini, G. (2020). Multiple functions of drawings. *Journal of urban design*, 26 (3), pp. 374-394, DOI: 10.1080/13574809.2020.1801341

Morosini, P. (2010). *Seven keys to imagination: Creating the future by imagining the unthinkable*. London: Marshall Cavendish.

Morse, C., & Wisocki, P. A. (1991). Residential factors in behavioral programming for elderly. In: P. Wisocki. A (ed.), *Handbook of clinical behavior therapy with the elderly client* (pp. 97-106). New York: Plenum Press.

Moser, N. (2009). How do I love thee? *HNR*, 50, https://historicalnovelsociety.org/reviews/how-do-i-love-thee/

Nagmoti, J. (2020). Communications in large classrooms: Issues, challenges, and solutions. In: S. C. Parija., & B. V. Adkoli (eds.), *Effective medical communication* (pp. 111-122). Singapore: Springer.

Nordkvelle, Y. (2017). The long march: The origins of voice, emotion and image in higher education. In: G. Jamissen., P. Hardy., Y. Nordkvellle., & H. Pleasants (eds.), *Digital storytelling in higher education: International perspectives* (pp. 1-11). Cham, Switzerland: Palgrave Macmillan.

Nørgaard, N., Montoro, R., & Busse, B. (2010). *Key terms in stylistics*. London: Continuum International Publishing Group.

Olsen, J., Saracci, R., & Trichopoulos, D. (2010). *Teaching epidemiology*. Oxford: Oxford U Press.

Opddecam, E., & Everaert, P. (2019). Choice-based learning: Lecture-based or team learning? *Accounting education*, 28 (3), pp. 239-273, DOI:10.1080/09639284.2019.1570857

Packer, S. (2002). *Dreams in myth, medicine, and movies*. Westport, Conn.: Praeger.

Panther, K., & Thornburg, L. L. (Eds.). (2003). *Metonymy and pragmatic inferencing*. Amsterdam: John Benjamins B.V.

Parsons, W., Talbot, F. X., & Walsh, G. G. (1983). *Thought*. New York: Fordham U Press.

Paz, A. (2011). *The power of faith: A journey to healing, wholeness, and harmony*. Bloomington, IN: iUniverse LLC.

Pöhlmann, S. (2015). *Future-founding poetry: Topographies of beginning from Whitman to the twenty-first century*. New York: Camden House.

Pomorska, K., & Rudy, S. (Eds.). (1987). *Roman Jakobson: Language in literature*. Cambridge, MA: Belknap Press.

Povoledo, E. (2013). Pope appeals for more interreligious dialogue. *The New York Times*, https://www.nytimes.com/2013/03/23/world/europe/pope-francis-urges-more-interreligious-dialogue.html

Pughe, B., & Philpot, T. (2007). *Living alongside a child's recovery: Therapeutic parenting with traumatized children*. London: Jessica Kingsley Publishers.

Rait, R. S. (1912). *Life in the medieval university*. Cambridge: Cambridge U Press.

Rao, N. (2011). *Style in journalism*. New Delhi: Readworthy.

Rashdall, H. (2010). *The universities of Europe in the middle ages* (vol. 1), pp. 206-232. Oxford: Clarendon Press.

Ray, M. K. (2018). *Studies in literary criticism*. New Delhi: Atlantic Publishers & Distributors Ltd.

Reah, D. (1998). *The language of newspapers*. London: Routledge.

Reisigl, M., & Wodak, R. (2009). The discourse-historical approach. In: R. Wodak., & M. Meyer (eds.), *Methods of critical discourse analysis* (pp. 87-121). London: Sage Publications Ltd.

Reston, J. (1963). 'I have a dream ...'; Peroration by Dr. King sums up a day the capital will remember. *The New York Times*, https://www.nytimes.com/1963/08/29/archives/i-have-a-dream-peroration-by-dr-king-sums-up-a-day-the-capital-will.html

Reynods, C. F. (2013). *Reflections on the past and the future*. Bloomington, IN: Xlibris LLC.

Ribière, M. (2008). *Barthes*. Penrith, CA: Humanities-Ebooks, LLP.

Risi, E., Pronzato, R., & Di Faia, G. (2021). Everything is inside the home: The boundaries of home confinement during the Italian lockdown. *European societies*, https://doi.org/10.1080/14616696.2020.1828977

Ritu, M. S. (2012). Ethnic cleansing in Myanmar. *The New York Times*, https://www.nytimes.com/interactive/2019/10/15/world/asia/myanmar-ethnic-cleansing.html

Rix, J., Nind, M., Simmons, K., & Sheehy, K. (2005). *Policy and power in inclusive education: Values into practice*. London: Routledge Falmer.

Robinson, P. (2002). *Poetry, poets, readers: Making things happen*. New York: Oxford U Press Inc.

Rogers, C., & Kutnick, P. (1992). *The social psychology of the primary school*. London: Routledge.

Rosenblatt, L. M. (1994). *The reader, the text, the poem: The transactional theory of the literary work*. Southern Illinois U.

--------------------. (2005). *Literature as exploration*. New York: The Modern Language Association of America.

Rothstein, D., & Santana, L. (2011). *Make just one change: Teach students to ask their own questions*. Cambridge: Harvard Education Press.

Rumi, J. M. (2010). *The Masnavi: The spiritual couplets of Maulana Jalalu'd-din Muhammad Rumi* (Trans. E. H. Whinfield). New York: Cosimo, Inc.

Ryan, H. R. (1995). *U.S. Presidents as orators: A bio-critical sourcebook*. Westport, Conn.: Greenwood Publishing Group, Inc.

Rymes, D. (2016). *Classroom discourse analysis: A tool for critical reflection*. New York: Routledge.

Sandquist, E. J. (2009). I have a dream. *King's dream* (pp. 229-234). New Haven & London: Yale U Press.

Sasnett, M. T., & Sepmeyer, I. H. (1966). *Educational systems of Africa: Interpretations for use in the evaluation of academic credentials*. Berkeley and Los Angeles: U of California Press.

Schapiro, M. (1961). Style. In: M. Philipson (ed.), *Aesthetics today* (pp 81-113). Cleveland, OH: World Publishing.

Schieble, M. B. (2010). Reading between the lines of reader response: Constructing 'the Other' through the aesthetic stance, *Changing English*, 17 (4), pp. 375- 384, DOI: 10.1080/1358684X.2010.528870

Schmitt, N., & Schmitt, D. (2020). *Vocabulary in language teaching*. Cambridge: Cambridge U Press.

Schupbach, W. (1982). The paradox of Rembrandt's anatomy of Dr. Tulp. *Med hist suppl*, 2, pp. 1–110, PMID: 6765286; PMCID: PMC2557395

Scott, A. O. (2010). Life during wartime. *The New York Times*, http://www.nytimes.com/2010/07/23/movies/23life.html

Scott, L. O. (2002). *James Baldwin's later fiction: Witness to the journey*. Michigan: Michigan State U.

Scott, S. (2008). *All our sisters: Stories of homeless women in Canada*. Ontario: Higher Education U of Toronto Press.

Seamonds, D. A. (1985). *Healing memories*. Wheaton, Ill.: Victor Books.

Senior, J. (2020). Happiness won't save you. *The New York Times*, https://www.nytimes.com/2020/11/24/opinion/happiness-depression-suicide-psychology.html

Shanahan, T. (2012). Developing fluency in the context of effective literacy instruction. In: T. Rasinski., C. Blachowicz, & K. Lems (eds.), *Fluency instruction: Research-based practices* (pp. 17-34). New York: The Guilford Press.

Sheehy, K. (2005). Inclusive education and ethical research. In: K. Sheehy, M. Nind., J. Rix., & K. Simmons (eds.), *Ethics and research in inclusive education: Values into practice* (pp. 1-6). New York: Routledge Falmer.

Shesgreen, S. (Ed.). (1973). Scholars at a lecture. *Engravings by Hogarth*. New York: Dover Publications, Inc.

Shi, Y., Peng, C., Wang, S., & Yang, H. H. (2018). The effects of smart classroom-based instruction on college students' learning engagement and internet self-efficacy. In: S. K. S. Cheung., L. Kwok., K. Kubota., L. Lee., & J. Tokito (eds.), *Blended learning: Enhancing learning success* (pp. 263-274). Osaka: Springer.

Shihipar, A. (2022). Are better things coming? Inshallah. *The New York Times*, https://www.nytimes.com/2022/01/25/magazine/inshallah.html

Short, M. (1996). *Exploring the language of poems, plays and prose*. London: Longman.

Showalter, G., & Monroe, J. (2020). *All write already*. Oklahoma: Author Talk Media LLC.

Siddiqi, I. H. (2010). *Indo-Persian historiography up to the thirteenth century*. New Delhi: Primus Books.

Simpson, P. (2004). *Stylistics: A resource book for students*. London and New York: Routledge.

Sorensen, J. T. (2012). *Optical allusions: Screens, paintings, and poetry in classical Japan (ca. 800-1200)*. Leiden, The Netherlands: Koninklijke Brill NV.

Stack, L. (2022). Why Ramadan generates millions in charitable giving every year. *The New York Times*, https://www.nytimes.com/2022/04/29/nyregion/ramadan-charitable-giving.html

Staff Writer. (2003). Muslims in European Schools. *The New Times*, https://www.nytimes.com/2003/10/08/opinion/muslims-in-european-schools.html

Sterling, C. H. (Ed.). (2009). *Encyclopedia of journalism*. Thousand Oaks, California: Sage Publications, Inc.

Stockwell, P. (2002). *Cognitive poetics: An introduction*. London and New York: Routledge.

---------------. (Ed.). (2007). *Language and linguistics: The key concepts*. New York: Routledge.

Sue, E., & Sue, B. A. (2019). *Intercultural communication: A Canadian perspective* (pp. 173- 202). Toronto, Ontario: Canadian Scholars.

Toswell, M. J. (2017). *Today's medieval university*. Leeds: Arc Humanities Press.

Tracy, S. C. (2002). *Langston Hughes and the Blues*. Champaign: U of Illinois Press.

Tyson, L. (2006). *Critical theory today: A user-friendly guide*. New York: Routledge.

Usher, N. (2014). *Making news at the New York Times*. Ann Arbor, Michigan: U of Michigan Press.

Valli, C., & Lucas, C. (2000). *Linguistics of American sign language: An introduction*. Washington, D.C.: Gallaudet U.

Van Dijk, L. A., & Jochems, W. M. G. (2002). Changing a traditional lecturing approach into an interactive approach: Effects of interrupting the monologue in lectures. *Int. engng ed*. 18 (3), pp. 275-284, https://www.ijee.ie/articles/Vol18-3/IJEE1300.pdf

Van Dijk, T. A. (1981). Discourse studies and education. *Applied linguistics*, II (1), pp. 1-26, https://doi.org/10.1093/applin/II.1.1

------------------. (2006). Discourse, context and cognition. *Discourse studies*. London, Thousand Oaks, CA and New Delhi: Sage Publications, 8 (1), pp. 159-177.

Van Hear, N. (2017). Imagining refugia. *Foreign policy*. https://www.foreignaffairs.com/articles/world/2017-10-17/imagining-refugia

Verdonk, P. (2002). *Stylistics*. New York: Oxford U Press.

Von Albrecht, M. (1997). *A history of Roman literature: From Livius Andronicus to Boethius: With special regard to its influence on world literature*. New York: E. J. Brill.

Von Oldershausen, S. (2021). How growing up in New York after 9/11 shaped these Muslim leaders. *The New York Times*, https://www.nytimes.com/2021/09/10/nyregion/sept-11-muslim-new-york.html

Wales, K. (2011). *A dictionary of stylistics*. New York: Routledge.

Wan, M. (2014). *Incidental trainer: A reference guide for training design, development, and delivery*. Boca Raton: Taylor & Francis Group.

Wanlace, W. S., & Prabhu, N. (1975). *English through reading*. Hong Kong: Macmillan Publishers Ltd.

Warriner, D., Anderson, K. T. (2017). Discourse analysis in educational research. In: K. King., Y. J. Lai., S. May. (eds.), *Research methods in language and education* (pp. 297-309). Cham., Switzerland: Springer, https://doi.org/10.1007/978-3-319-02249-9_22

Washington, D. A. (2015). I have a dream: A rhetorical analysis. *The black scholar*, 23 (2), pp. 16-19, DOI: 10.1080/00064246.1993.11413090

Weingarten, H. P. (2021). Why are Canadian universities so slow to innovate. *Nothing less than great: Reforming Canada's universities* (pp. 103-119). Toronto: U of Toronto Press.

Wellington, J., & Ireson, G. (2013). *Science learning, science teaching*. New York: Routledge.

Whippman, R. (2017). Happiness is other people. *The New York Times*, https://www.nytimes.com/2017/10/27/opinion/sunday/happiness-is-other-people.html

Whiteley, S., & Canning, P. (2017). Reader response research in stylistics. *Language and literature*, 26 (2), pp. 71-87.

Wormeli, R. (2009). *Metaphors & analogies: Power tools for teaching any subject*. Grandview Heights, OH: Stenhouse Publishers.

Wright, W. M. (2009). *Rhetoric and theology*. Berlin: Walter de Gruyter GmbH & Co. KG.

Zeng, H. L., Chen, D. X., Li, Q., & Wang, X. Y. (2020). Effects of seminar teaching method versus lecture-based learning in medical education: A meta-analysis of randomized controlled trials. *Medical teacher*, 42 (12), pp. 1334-1349, DOI:10.1080/0142159X.2020.18051

Answer Key

CHAPTER 1: STYLE AND THE POETIC EXPRESSION

1) Style refers to any specific way of using language, which is characteristic of an author, school, period, or genre. Particular styles may be defined by their diction, syntax, imagery, rhythm, as well as the use of figures, or by any other linguistic feature. It is worth mentioning that some categories of style have been named after certain authors (e.g. Ciceronian), periods (e.g. Augustan), and professions (e.g. journalistic), while in the Renaissance a scheme of three stylistic levels was adopted, distinguishing the high or 'grand' style from the middle or 'mean' style and the low or 'base' style [For further details, see Baldick, C. (2001). *The concise Oxford dictionary of literary terms.* New York: Oxford U Press, p. 247].

2) Stylisticians have approached style in different ways owing to the diversity of intellectual schools and literary movements that yielded inconsistent readings to texts. To set an example, the style adopted by the Neo-classicists, apart from its mission in delighting and instructing, depicted the 'Age of Reason', which gave priority to clarity, order, rationality and called for general truths rather than particular insights.

3) Both. It can be abstract (ideas / feelings); it can be concrete (when those ideas and feelings are articulated in spoken and written language). Other examples can include fashion, architecture, publicity, etc. (i.e. how fashion designers, architects and advertisers conceptualize their products before translating them as real objects in the real world).

4) Style for the Romantics has to do with imagination and it involves natural elements such as the moon, trees, nightingales, etc. It is bound up with ethics and morality. The Romantics focused on the heart because it is the provenance of human feelings and emotions; by contrast, the Neo-classicists focused on the power of the mind and the intellect as they endow them with the ability to think and reason in systematic ways. Two examples are suggested here: William Wordsworth's "I Wandered Lonely as a Cloud"; Alexander Pope's "Essay on Man." In the first, Wordsworth engages with memory and nature as the poet meditates and rejoices over seeing daffodils in the woods, which revived his spirit in nature. In the

second, Pope proposed a system of ethics and the idea that the Universe, as one perfect creation of God, operates in a rational fashion according to natural regulations.

5) Style has to do with aesthetics and ornamentation; it can also be described as embellishment, which incessantly aims to move people and get them to respond immediately and appropriately.

6) Three features could be thought of:
    a. word order
    b. clever use of metaphors
    c. rhyme

CHAPTER 2: SEMANTIC AND PRAGMATIC MEANINGS IN "ABOU BEN ADHEM"

1) The central themes of the poem have to do with love, fellowship, peace and devotion to humanity. Other sub-themes relate to co-existence, intercultural dialogue, kindness and self-abnegation.

2) Probably because Abou had abdicated his worldly fortunes and chosen asceticism as a style of life. It is a compelling piece of writing due to the presence of metaphors and other stylistic tropes such as sound patterning, simile and story-telling.

3) In the poem, foregrounding takes multiple forms: parallelism (e.g. the angel wrote / and vanished); deviation from norm (e.g. Awoke one night) along with repetitions (e.g. Abou Ben Adhem, Ben Adhem, Abou).

4) Simile (e.g. like a lily in bloom); personification (e.g. the Vision raised its head); hyperbole (e.g. a book of gold); alliteration (e.g. love the lord); invocation (e.g. may his tribe increase!).

5) As the major themes of the poem are love, fellowship, peace and commitment to humanity, I think the poem can be taught in multicultural classrooms to encourage students to observe esteem and respect for people of different cultures.

CHAPTER 3: CONCEPTUAL METAPHORS AND RHETORIC: "HOW DO I LOVE THEE?"

1) Probably to make the articulation of love more logical and quite reasonable.

2) I think if the title was written in the declarative form, the impact of the poem would not be the same. The rhetorical question is very provocative as it stimulates deep reflection.

Answer Key

3) For example, [Line 12]. This particular line betrays the integrity of the speaker and her loyalty to the addressee.

4) It is always hard to talk about abstract concepts such as "love" and "breath" because they demand acumen, honesty, and profound reflection.

5) With the exception of the archaic pronoun "thee", which might pose problems for some readers, the style is not challenging when we consider the question and immediate answer structured in the title of the poem.

6) Yes, since human beings tend to resort to metaphors to vehicle what they cannot say in ordinary language to others.

CHAPTER 4: A TRANSITIVITY PROCESS ANALYSIS OF "MANNERS"

1) In SFG, transitivity is regarded as one scientific method by which students can analyze separate clauses or clauses in contexts, and it is different from the traditional view of transitivity, which is a property of verb – whether it can take an abject(s) or not.

2) Transitivity analysis raises students' awareness of the basic constituents of the clause; so they can look at meaning from a critical lens. For example, they can detect which participant wields more power in discourse, whether the writer/speaker favours a specific gender over another, and whether he or she focuses more on action than on emotion or cognition.

3) As previously noted, transitivity analysis opens students' eyes to the workings of language and discourse; it enables them to detect ideologies and hidden meanings (i.e. choice of specific verb processes, circumstances and pronouns, etc.).

4) Existential process clauses were not considered by the poet. By contrast, material process clauses get the lion's share because manners require actions and not just words.

5) The symbols of the mare and the crow make the poem rich in meanings and interpretations; they add to it another colour so that it will not be sterile or impotent. If they were not included, it would sound less catchy in terms of imagery and metaphors.

6) Examples may include but not limited to the following poems: "The Raven" by Edgar Allan Poe (1809-1849); "She Sighs a Bird – She Chuckles" by Emily Dickinson (1830-1886); "Baby Tortoise" by D.H. Lawrence (1885-1930), etc.

CHAPTER 5: AN ABERRANT DECODING OF "MEMORY"

1) Ephemerality; appearances; memory; charm; inner vs. outer beauty.

2) Probably because he saw that people were easily trapped by physicality and did not value other treasures which their compatriots possess.

3) Of course. The first deals with the explicit / literal meaning while the second deals with the implicit and pragmatic meaning. To illustrate, an open hand refers to the human hand, but it can also signify generosity and an act of giving. Also, a candle can indicate a stick of wax that provides light / fragrance, but it can be a symbol of holy illumination and self-sacrifice.

4) Preferred reading is also called the dominant reading; it is the meaning that is imposed by the writer/speaker. The literary approach corresponding to this sort of reading is called the intentional approach (For further details, see Hall, 1980).

5) "Nymph of the Garden Where all Beauties Be" by Sir Philip Sidney; "Sonnet 54" by William Shakespeare; "She Walks in Beauty" by Lord Byron; "Hymn to Intellectual Beauty" by Percy Bysshe Shelley; "Essential Beauty" by Philip Larkin, etc.

6) This is how I myself paraphrased Yeats' poem "Memory":

> All people have lovely faces
> And all of them have charm
> Yet charm and face won't last
> Because they leave like hares so fast
> Not like this healing honest heart.

Though hard and challenging, I think the experience of poetry writing is pleasurable and so rewarding.

CHAPTER 6: AFRO-AMERICAN "DREAMS": A CONSTRUCTIVIST APPROACH

1) Because dreams help people move ahead.

2) Maybe inequality and discrimination.

3) The style of the poem is quite simple and within the reach of the average reader.

4) Apart from being short and concise, the two poems have invested on the power of metaphors; however, they addressed different themes.

5) Speaking for myself, I agree that multiple voices are included in "Dreams" on account of the use of the imperative form. The speaker is reaching out to the reader with the intention of cherishing the same dreams and aspirations.

CHAPTER 7: READER-RESPONSE THEORY: EXPLORING STUDENTS' SENSE OF CREATIVITY

1) Reader-response theory is a school of literary theory which focuses attention primarily on the reader (or "audience") and their experience of texts, whether they are literary or non-literary.

2) Reception theory is a form of reader-response criticism that is associated with the Konstance School of *Reception kritik* and the work of Hans Robert **Jauss** and Wolfgang **Iser**. Reception theory is concerned with both the aesthetic and the historical aspect of reading, i.e. the ways in which readers use texts for pleasure, and how readings alter and shift through history. Iser distinguishes these two strands by claiming that 'A theory of response has its roots in the text; a theory of reception arises from a history of readers' judgements [For more details, see Malpas, S., & Wake, P. (2013). The *Routledge companion to critical and cultural theory*. London: Routledge, p. 287].

3) It is the poetry that boosts up their morale and leads them to pursue paths of positive change in their lives.

4) When students can respond to poetry through poetry, we can say they developed a sense of creativity.

5) Teachers should use the reader-response approach in L2 because it alters students' negative attitudes of texts and encourages them to enjoy and appreciate world literature. When they activate their background knowledge, or they revisit their typical life experiences, their diverging emotions and cultural values, and when they find suitable links and adequate connections between the world of the text and their own worlds, the text itself becomes both impactful and more meaningful to them.

6) The question of validity and objectivity of interpretations still pose a serious problem to researchers and teachers who endorse reader-response theory.

CHAPTER 8: THE PANDEMIC HOME IN PANDEMIC POETRY: "AND THE PEOPLE STAYED HOME"

1) Exercising, resting, listening, praying, making art, playing and meditating.

2) Because the public space was closed and it was recommended that people stay at their homes. As a result, they practised a wide range of rituals together, which help establish a sense of friendship and unity within the family system.

3) For example, "At Home" by Christina Rossetti (1830-1894); "Home" by Edward Thomas (1878-1917); "A Child's Garden" by Rudyard Kipling (1865-1936), etc.

4) Mind style can be defined as people's mental perceptions of the world.

5) Yes, because several people across the globe have explored themselves in the pandemic home and were able to climb Maslow's pyramid of hierarchy needs. Not only did they find love, shelter, belonging and esteem, but they also reached their full potentials. Students, for instance, have won prizes when they participated in virtual competitions on creative reading and writing from their pandemic homes.

6) In my opinion, the target audience of the poem is every individual who experienced self-quarantine during the last global lockdown. Note the simplicity of language used, the theme of the poem, and the diverse activities that are highlighted by the poet.

CHAPTER 9: LECTURING AND LEARNING STYLES: "A MEDIEVAL CLASSROOM"

1) *a. Advantages*

- It is economical.
- It gives factual information.
- It hones students' speaking skills.

b. Disadvantages

- Tactile learners might be distracted.
- Instead of becoming producers of knowledge, students turn into consumers of information.
- Not all students are involved.

Answer Key 153

2) As said, this method does not appeal to all learners, especially tactile ones. It might be suitable for the auditory and visually-oriented students.

3) The classroom discourse is predicated on the teacher's ability to lecture from a podium to different learners, all of whom exhibit various styles of learning and information processing. The teacher is viewed as the source of knowledge -- the sage on the stage.

4) In fact, different aspects are foregrounded, and these include: teacher's character students' engagement in the lecture, forms of distraction, etc.

5) Yes, I agree. The lecture-based method is more suitable for auditory learners since they are seen as active listeners, who process information through the hearing sense.

CHAPTER 10: STUDENTS' VOICES ABOUT HEADLINES AND BLURBS

1) Headlines can have the following features: ellipsis, allusion, nominalization, capitalization.

2) The blurb gives a summary of the book and it usually includes statements by outstanding scholars and well-established authors.

3) Both genres dwell on ellipsis, intertextuality and allusions to other texts.

4) Arguably, the purpose of headlines is not only to inform but also to persuade the readers to purchase the newspaper.

5) Students can examine aspects such as register (i.e., field, tenor and mode); alliteration; typography and graphology; nominal structures; ellipsis; intertextuality; deixis; rhetorical questions, etc.

6) I suggest that students discuss the theme of the two blurbs, use their common ground knowledge, explore context, examine lexical and grammatical categories and conclude with their overall impressions about them. And to make their analysis more scientific, they need raise at least two pertinent questions, use technical terms and refer to theories and principles governing the field of Stylistics.

CHAPTER 11: RHETORICAL TROPES: "THE NEW YORK TIMES"

1) According to Roman Jakobson, language has six functions: Referential, Emotive, Conative, Phatic, Metalingual and Poetic.

2) For M. Halliday, language plays three metafunctions: the Ideational, the Interpersonal and the Textual.

3) As I see it, the rhetorical devices empower and embellish human discourse; they can serve quite well the purpose of persuasion.
4) Highly rhetorical, eloquent and persuasive.
5) Given that style is personal and abstract, it relates to performance as it propels language users, writers or speakers, to select their expressions among the wide range of alternatives made available to them by their linguistic competence.

Glossary

Abou Ben Adhem – (d. 875) is one of the most celebrated mystic saints of Islam, and he was originally Prince of the city of Balkh. His life caught the attention of Western scholars because he was a wealthy king having control of the riches of several provinces. He renounced his throne and hankered after a humble lifestyle based on solitude and asceticism. A gladsome story told by him runs as follows: "One night I saw in a dream Gabriel, with a piece of paper in his hand. 'What are you doing?' I asked him. 'I am writing on this sheet of paper the names of the friends of the Lord.' 'Will you write mine among them?' Ibrahim asked. 'But you are not one of His friends.' 'If I am not one of His friends, at least I am a friend of His friends.' Immediately a Voice was heard, 'O Gabriel, write Ibrahim's name on the first line, for he who loves Our friends is Our friend.'" [For more details, see Griffiths, F. (1910). *Mystics and saints of Islam*. London: Francis Griffiths, pp. 36-45].

Edward Said – (1935-2003) was an outstanding scholar, public intellectual and a well-known cultural critic. As a Palestinian American, he worked as a Professor of literature at Columbia University and applied both his knowledge and bi-cultural background to explain the wide fissures between the West and the East. He is widely recognized for his initiation of the field of postcolonial studies, which critiques the myths, fallacies and misrepresentations about the Other in Western art and literature. Said's major influences were philosophers such as Michel Foucault, Franz Fanon and Antonio Gramsci. His most popular works are *Orientalism* (1978), *The World, the Text and Critic* (1983) and *Culture and Imperialism* (1993).

Elisabeth Barrett Browning – (1806-1861) was an English poet, widely known both in Britain and the United States of America. From an early age, she wrote poetry and produced both prose and translation, notwithstanding her frail health and physical problems. Besides, she not only contributed to the abolition of slavery but also participated in reforming child labour legislation. Her volume entitled *Poems* (1844) granted her much fame and popularity, and it allowed her to be acquainted with poet Robert Browning, with whom she engaged in secret courtship and legal marriage since her father was not in favour of it. Her famous poetic writings, including "How Do I Love Thee?" (1845) and *Aurora Leigh* (1856), had a tremendous impact on the late American poets such as Emily Dickinson and Edgar Allan Poe.

Elisabeth Bishop – (1911-1979) was an American poet and a woman of letters originating from Worcester (Massachusetts). She served as a consultant in the Poetry to the Library of Congress from 1949 to 1950; she received many prizes and awards for her poetry gifts and creative productions. Among her books, one can cite *North & South*, which was published in 1946, *Questions of Travel* (1965), *The Complete Poems* (1969) and *Geography III* (1977). As a teacher, Bishop has been lecturing at many university institutions, such as the University of Washington and Harvard, before she taught at the Massachussetts Institute of Technology (MIT).

Ezra Pound – (1885-1972) was an expatriate American critic and poet, who taught both French and Spanish. He is considered one of the precursors of the modernist poetry movement, which saw light between 1890 and 1950. His major contribution lies in his ability to develop imagism – an approach to poetry that emphasized the economy of language, conciseness and precision in the poetic expression. His most influential books include *Exultations* (1909), *Provenca* (1910), *Lustra and Other Poems* (1917), along with *Patria Mia* (1950) and *The Cantos* (1972).

Gibran Khalil Gibran – (1883-1931) was a Lebanese American poet, philosopher, visual artist and writer. He is famous for his ground-breaking work *The Prophet* (1923), a book comprising about 26 fables, all of which were translated into more than 100 languages. He was one of the best-selling authors in the United States of America and beyond. His other popular works include *The Madman* (1918) and *The Earth Gods* (1931), to mention but these two.

Gilles Deleuze – (1925-1995) was a French philosopher, who made many important contributions to literature, philosophy, literary theory, fine art and film analysis. He consecrated his efforts to the examination of the thoughts and ideas of several philosophers like Kant, Nietzsche, Spinoza, the Stoics, Hume and Leibniz. The works that made him so popular in the Western world are *Capitalism and Schizophrenia: Anti- Oedipus* (1972) and *A Thousand Plateau* (1980), both of which were co-authored with the French semiotician and psychoanalyst Félix Guattari. His magnum opus is *Difference and Repetition* (1968).

Julia Kristeva – (b. 1941) was a Bulgarian and French semiotician, novelist, literary critic and psychoanalyst. She has been celebrated in different universities worldwide on account of her prolific and sound critical productions on philosophy, literary theory, feminism and cultural studies. Her works have opened a wide range of perspectives in the study of the ways in which human beings write and communicate. Among the books that she authored and which have been rendered from French into English, there are, for instance, *Séméiôtiké: Recherches pour une Sémanalyse (Desire in Language: A Semiotic Approach to Literature* and *Art and La Revolution Du Langage Poétique (Revolution in Poetic Language)*.

Glossary 157

Kitty O'Meara – is an American retired teacher, whose prose poem, "And the People Stayed Home", has been shared thousand times on social media by people of all walks of life and cultural backgrounds. She never thought that her poem will be received by a large public and trigger both healing and hope in people despite the burdens and hurdles of the global lockdown and the COVID-19 pandemic. She was dubbed the "poet laureate of the pandemic" by *O, the Oprah Magazine* that was created by the celebrity talk-show host Oprah Winfrey and Hearst Communications.

Ivor Armstrong Richards – (1893-1979) is famously known as I.A. Richards. He was an English poet, educator and literary critic. His work has influenced New Criticism, a formalist movement that focused on the close reading of a literary text, especially poetry. His objective was to discover how a work of literature functions as a self-referential and self-contained aesthetic object. His seminal books such as *Principles of Literary Criticism* (1924), *Practical Criticism* (1929) and *The Philosophy of Rhetoric* (1936) have all contributed to the establishment of the literary methodology of the New Criticism.

Langston Hughes – (1901-1967) was an African American novelist, poet and social activist, best known for his leadership of the Harlem Renaissance – a cultural and intellectual movement that sought to revive African and American heritage in terms of dance, fashion, literature, music and the like; he is considered by many critics as the precursor of jazz poetry, with jazz music and the jazz environment as its subject. Throughout his life, he practiced different jobs and travelled across Africa and Europe working as a seaman, an experience that burnished his artistic talents and poetic intelligence with regards to African American literature in the 1920.

Laurentius de Voltolina – (1350-1400?) – was an Italian painter who became famous for capturing an illustration of a medieval university classroom at the prestigious University of Bologna (ca. 1380). His painting is entitled, *Liber des Henricus de Alemania*, and it displays Professor Henricus de Alemannia lecturing to a group of students. Whereas some of them were fully engaged, others -- especially those sitting in the back row -- were talking among themselves and felt disengaged.

Leigh Hunt – (1784-1859) was a critic, poet and essayist, whose writing led to the thriving of the Romantic movement in England. His poetry encompassed a wide range of styles and forms like satires, odes, narrative poems, sonnets and translations from other languages, notably Greek, French, Roman and Italian. As a supporter of poets Percy Bysshe Shelley and John Keats, Hunt has antedated the Aesthetic Movement when he initiated the idea of "poetry for its own sake." His poetry volumes involve *Story of Rimini* (1816); *Foliage* (1818); *Hero and Leander*, and *Bacchus and*

Ariadne (1819), yet he is famous for his popular poems "Jenny kiss'd Me" (1838) and "Abou Ben Adhem" (1834).

Louise Rosenblatt – (1904-2005) was an American Professor, best known for her academic research on the teaching and learning of literature. Like all leading theorists who embraced the ethos of reader-response theory and criticism, she exhibited a keen interest in readers' unique reactions and responses to a given text. Her most influential and pioneering book is *The Reader, The Text, The Poem: The Transactional Theory of the Literary Work* (1978; 1994), in which she suggested that the act of reading literature involves a "transaction" between the reader and the text. Meaning, for her, does not reside in the written work itself (often called "a poem" in her writing) but in the reader's "transaction" with it. Each "transaction" is seen as a unique experience that allows the text and the reader to interact and influence each other continuously.

Martin Luther King Jr. – (1929-1968) was an American activist, minister and leader of the civil rights movement. Since 1955, he led the civil rights movement and attempted to end the poverty and segregation of African Americans in many parts of the United States and across the globe. Inspired by his Christian background and the non-violent doctrine of Mahatma Ghandi, Luther King drew on the power of words and eloquent speech to achieve racial equality through peaceful resistance and non-violent discourse. In 1964, he was awarded the Nobel Peace Prize. After his assassination by gunshot in 1968, he was offered the Presidential Medal of Freedom (1977) and Congressional Gold Medal (2004).

Michael Bakhtin – (1895-1975) was a Russian scholar and literary critic. He did much work on ethics, literary theory and the philosophy of language. His writings have inspired many thinkers and intellectual movements; they circulated widely in various disciplines such as philosophy, sociology, anthropology, history, psychology, literary criticism, to mention but a few. His notable books are *Problems of Dostoevsky's Poetics* (1963), *Questions of Literature and Aesthetics* (1975) and *Rabelais and His World* (1968).

Michael Halliday – (1925 – 2018) was a British applied linguist, educationist and university Professor; he is considered the founding father of Systemic Functional Linguistics (SFL), in which he regarded language as a social phenomenon. He was also interested in the work of intonation, child development, the linguistic study of literary texts, the construction of knowledge, scientific English and discourse analysis. Before he studied linguistics in China and received his doctorate at Cambridge University, he had studied Chinese language and culture. His major published works addressed a variety of topics; they included but were not limited to

Explorations in the Functions of Language (1973); *Learning How to Mean* (1975); *An Introduction to Functional Grammar* (2004).

Percy Bysshe Shelley – (1792 -1822) was an English Romantic poet who influenced enormously poets like Robert Browning, Thomas Hardy and W.B. Yeats. He is remembered for his mastery of poetry genres, imagery as well as verse forms. His best-known works include "Ozymandias" (1818), "Ode to the West Wind" (1819), and "To a Skylark" (1820). He also wrote many controversial essays on social, religious, political and philosophical issues that appeal to some historical figures such as Mahatma Gandhi and George Barnard Shaw.

Ralph Waldo Emerson – (1803-1882) was an American philosopher, poet and essayist. He is deemed as the founding father of the Transcendentalist movement -- a cultural literary, spiritual and philosophical movement, which thrived in the New England region, emphasizing, on the one hand, the inherent goodness of nature and humanity and on the other hand underscoring the idea of a personal knowledge of God. Emerson was influenced by Eastern and Western poets such as Samuel Taylor Coleridge, William Wordsworth, Saadi, Hafez, and others. Among his highly celebrated works, one can cite *Nature, Society and Solitude, Poems, The Conduct of Life*, along with individual essays such as "The Over-Soul"; "Self-Reliance"; "Saadi", etc.

Robert Browning – (1812-1889) was an English playwright and poet who excelled in the use of characterization, challenging syntax, irony and dark humour, especially in dramatic monologues. After his death, he was viewed as a philosopher and wise man since he enriched the Victorian social and political discourse with insightful thoughts and ideas. He is well recognized for poems like "Pauline", 'Paracelsus", "Sordello", among others. In 1846, he married his fellow poet, Elisabeth Barrett Browning, and the couple settled in Italy.

Roland Barthes – (1915-1980) was a French literary critic, theorist and semiologist. He is well-known for his 1967 essay, "The Death of the Author," which critiqued old approaches used in literary criticism. Most of his works focused on the examination of a wide range of sign systems that were prevalent in Western popular culture. They also influenced the evolution of several theories, such as anthropology, literary theory, structuralism and post-structuralism.

Roman Jakobson – (1896-1982) was a Russian-American thinker, literary theorist and linguist. He is seen as the most influential linguist of the twentieth century since he developed a structural analysis of language, art and poetry. He is credited with the identification of the functions of language: referential (= contextual information); poetic (= autotelic); emotive (= self-expression); conative (= vocative or imperative addressing of receiver); phatic (= checking channel working); metalingual (= checking code of working) [For more details, see Middleton, R. (1990). *Studying popular music*. Philadelphia: Open U Press, p. 241]. His groundbreaking works are *Child Language, Aphasia and Phonological Universals* (1941); *Style in Language* (1960); *The Framework of Language* (1980). Among the theorists that have been decisively influenced by him, we can mention Claude Lévi-Strauss, Roland Barthes and Noam Chomsky.

Rumi – (1207-1273), well-known by the honorific Mawlānā, was a great Sufi poet, Muslim theologian, and mystic scholar who inspired world literature and mystical thought with his didactic poem *The Masnavi*, which comprises more than 26,000 verses, teaching Sufis how to attain their spiritual goal of being in love with God. His enormous influence went far beyond national, ethnic and religious boundaries since his odes, texts and poems were rendered into many world languages and were appreciated by Muslims and non-Muslims. Before he founded the Mawlawiya Sufi path, he had met the dervish Shams-e Tabrizi, who transformed his life completely and led him to the way of asceticism and Sufism.

Samuel Taylor Coleridge – (1772-1834) was an English philosopher, literary critic and poet. Together with his close friend William Wordsworth, he founded the Romantic school of thought in England. He had exerted a great influence on thinkers like Ralph Waldo Emerson and on the American Transcendentalist movement of the nineteenth century. He is highly celebrated in the Anglophone world since he wrote many influential and inspiring pieces of literary criticism such as *Biographia Literaria* (1817), which sketches his opinions and literary life. Besides, he was able to introduce German idealist philosophy in his home country, and he is nowadays best known for his two long poems, *The Rime of the Ancient Mariner* (1798) and *Kubla Khan* (1816).

Stuart Hall – (1932-2014) was a Jamaican-born British cultural theorist, sociologist and political activist. With the collaboration of Richard Hoggard and Raymond Williams, he founded the school of thought known by the name Cultural Studies at Birmingham University. Thanks to his efforts and inspiration from the renowned French theorist Michel Foucault, the scope of cultural studies has been expanded to cover issues such as gender, ideology and race. He wrote numerous essays and books on Marx, Class, Gramsci, Ethnicity, Media, yet he is famous for his encoding and decoding model, resistance, questions of cultural identity, as well as the binary of West and the Rest. His published works include, for instance, *Deviancy, Politics and the Media* (1971); *Encoding and Decoding in the Television*

Discourse (1973); *The Hard Road to Renewal; Thatcherism and the Crisis of the Left* (1988)

T.S Eliot – (1888-1965) was an American-born British essayist, poet, playwright and publisher He is a prominent figure in modernist poetry. In 1927, he received his British citizenship. It was in London where he met his contemporary Ezra Pound, who helped him publish his most popular poem, "The Love Song of J. Alfred Prufrock" (1915) in *Poetry: A Magazine of Verse*. The poem, which was initially regarded as outlandish, attracted the attention of several literary critics worldwide. Other long poems made Eliot renowned in Britain and America, namely *The Waste Land* (1922), "Ash Wednesday" (1930), among others. In 1948, he was awarded the Nobel Prize in literature.

Umberto Eco – (1932-2016) was an Italian philosopher, novelist, semiotician and cultural critic. He is famous for his 1980 debut novel, *The Name of the Rose*, which is an intellectual mystery mixing up biblical analysis, medieval studies, literary theory with semiotics in fiction. He compiled a number of works reserved exclusively for children, along with translations from French and English. As an Emeritus Professor, he lectured at the oldest University of Bologna in Italy. His published books encompass works such as *A Theory of Semiotics* (1979); *Semiotics and the Theory of Language* (1986); *The Limits of Interpretation* (1994).

Victor Shklovsky – (1893-1934) was a Russian critic, writer and literary theorist. He is one of the most influential figures of Formalism, an innovative school of literary criticism that saw light in the twentieth century. He is famous for his concept of defamiliarization (*ostranenie*), which is so popular in Stylistics and the study of literature. Shklovsky staunchly believed that the latter's importance resides not in its social content but rather in its autonomous creation of language. His major pioneering works involve *Knight's Move* (1923); *Theory of Prose* (1925); *Leo Tolstoy* (1963).

William Butler Yeats – (1865-1939) was an Irish storyteller, dramatist, novelist and poet, whose poetry grew realistic and politicized as it subsumed Irish symbols and scenes. From an early age, he showed a penchant for poetry and studied Irish legends and the occult. To many critics, he was a symbolist poet since he was fond of allusive imagery and vague structures throughout his writing career. His symbols are not only physical but also immaterial, as they point to eternity and timelessness. His famous poems are "Byzantium", "Among School Children"; "Beggar to Beggar Cried"; "A Coat"; "A Dialogue of Self and Soul"; "The Four Ages of Man."

William Wordsworth – (1770-1850) was an English Romantic poet who contributed alongside Samuel Taylor Coleridge to the development and prosperity of the Romantic Movement in English literature with their co-authored collection of poems entitled, *Lyrical Ballads* (1798). He is widely recognized as a poet who is concerned with human connection to nature and a user of speech patterns and vocabulary related to everyday conversations. His most popular poems, including for instance, "I Wandered Lonely as a Cloud" or "Daffodils" (1807), "The World Is Too Much with Us" (c. 1802) and "She Dwelt Among the Untrodden Ways" (1800), cover a wide range of references to nature, love, solitude, and sharp criticism to materialism and industrialization as it caused environment degradation.

Wolfgang Iser – (1926-2007) was a German scholar who is highly acclaimed for his contributions to reader-response criticism in literary theory. Together with his compatriot Hans Robert Jauss, he is considered the precursor of the Constance School of reception theory, a version of reader-response theory that stresses each reader's reception or interpretation in deriving meaning from a literary text. For him, meaning is not a fixed object to be found within a text, but is rather an event of construction that happens somewhere in the interaction between the reader and the text. His major works include *Prospecting: From Reader Response to Literary Anthropology* (1989), *The Range of Interpretation* (2000) and *How to Do Theory* (2006).

Index

A

Abercrombie, 4, 133
academic, xiii, xv, 8, 131, 135, 137, 140, 143, 158
actor, 8
addressee, 8, 121, 129, 149
adjective, 8
Aggarwal, 8, 133
alliteration, 5, 8, 106, 117, 148, 153
allusion, 8, 104, 153
anaphora, 8, 118
Anderson, xiv, 8, 133, 145
angel, 5, 8, 148
Applegate, 101, 133
approach, xiv, xvi, 5, 8, 96, 106, 110, 113, 117, 129, 130, 131, 138, 141, 143, 145, 150, 151, 156
Aristotle, 4, 8, 136
art, xvi, 4, 7, 8, 94, 97, 113, 127, 134, 136, 152, 155, 156, 159
article, 8, 102, 103
Atkinson, 8, 134
attribute, 8
audience, 7, 8, 106, 113, 121, 126, 139, 151, 152
Austin, 8, 134
Azuike, 5, 134

B

Baker, 4, 134, 135
Bakhtin, 8, 119, 134, 158
Barthes, 8, 134, 143, 159, 160
beauty, xv, 7, 8, 130, 138, 150

Ben Adhem, xv, 8, 129, 148, 155, 158
Benson, 8, 134
Bishop, 8, 134, 155
blurb, xiii, xvi, 101, 106, 107, 108, 109, 111, 153
Branston, 8, 135
breath, 8, 149
broadsheet, 115, 116
Brown, 8, 114, 135
Browning, xv, 8, 140, 155, 159
Buckenmeyer, 8, 135

C

character, 6, 8, 153
choice, xv, 4, 5, 8, 96, 103, 104, 108, 113, 114, 131, 149
circumstance, 8
classroom, xiv, xvi, 8, 93, 95, 96, 97, 98, 101, 130, 131, 134, 137, 141, 144, 153, 157
clause, 8, 108, 118, 120, 126, 149
cohesion, 8, 107, 109, 118
Coleridge, 6, 7, 159, 160, 161
communication, xiv, xv, 8, 94, 95, 114, 115, 135, 140, 141, 142, 145
connotation, xvi, 8
content, xiii, 5, 8, 104, 106, 110, 113, 127, 161
context, 5, 8, 96, 102, 104, 108, 136, 138, 139, 144, 145, 153
cooperative principle, xv, 8, 129
coordinating conjunction, 8, 123
creativity, xvi, xvii, 8, 104, 151
culture, 5, 7, 8, 134, 138, 158, 159

D

defamiliarization, 161
Deleuze, 8, 136, 156
denotation, xvi, 8
dialogism, xvi, 8, 130
Dickinson, 8, 149, 155
Diffey, 6, 136
direct speech, 8
discourse, xiv, xvi, 8, 98, 102, 107, 108, 109, 110, 113, 114, 115, 116, 117, 120, 122, 124, 127, 128, 130, 131, 134, 135, 138, 143, 149, 153, 154, 158, 159
dream, 8, 118, 119, 133, 141, 143, 145, 155
dualist, 3, 4
Durant, 8, 136

E

Eco, 136, 161
education, 8, 95, 96, 97, 98, 110, 133, 134, 136, 137, 138, 139, 140, 141, 142, 143, 144, 145, 146
effect, 8, 110, 117, 121, 123
Eisner, 8, 136
Eliot, 8, 136, 161
Ellece, 4, 134
ellipsis, 101, 102, 103, 105, 108, 118, 153
Emerson, 6, 8, 134, 136, 159, 160
Entwistle, 94, 97, 137

F

face, xvi, 4, 5, 8, 120, 130, 150
Fairclough, 8, 137
family, ix, 8, 118, 119, 152
fellowship, 8, 148
field, 8, 153, 155
Fihriya, 8

Flowerdew, vii, 8, 137
foregrounding, 8, 117, 148
form, 4, 5, 7, 8, 104, 105, 117, 118, 122, 124, 127, 138, 148, 151
Fowler, 8, 137
Freud, 8, 137
function, 8, 95, 106, 108, 114, 117, 120, 122

G

genre, xv, xvi, 6, 7, 8, 115, 147
Gibran, 8, 156
goal, 8, 113, 130, 160
Gordon, 137
grammar, 8, 117, 136, 137, 138, 140
Granath, xv, 137
Grice, 8, 137

H

Hafez, 159
Hall, 8, 138, 150, 160
Halliday, 8, 94, 114, 120, 138, 141, 153, 158
Hark, 8
Harris-Moore, 8, 138
headline, xiii, 102, 103, 104, 105, 121, 122
healing, xvi, 7, 8, 130, 135, 137, 141, 142, 150, 157
Henricus, vii, ix, 8, 157
hierarchy need, vii, 8, 130, 152
Hippias, 8, 133
history, 8, 111, 123, 126, 135, 136, 138, 139, 145, 151, 158
home, xv, xvi, 8, 124, 130, 133, 134, 136, 137, 139, 140, 143, 152, 160
honorific, 160
horizontal, 8, 129
Hughes, xv, xvi, 8, 115, 139, 145, 157

human, xiii, xiv, xv, xvi, xvii, 6, 8, 107, 113, 115, 116, 119, 120, 123, 125, 129, 130, 131, 135, 136, 138, 141, 147, 149, 150, 154, 156, 162
Hunt, xv, 8, 129, 139, 157

I

image, 8, 93, 104, 105, 118, 140, 142
imagination, xv, 6, 8, 93, 104, 105, 136, 142, 147
indexicality, xv, 8
information, 8, 94, 95, 103, 108, 109, 113, 114, 127, 131, 141, 152, 153, 160
inspiration, 6, 8, 160
intelligence, 8, 157
interpersonal, 8, 93, 95
interpretation, 8, 102, 103, 104, 139, 162
intertextuality, xvi, 8, 101, 104, 105, 118, 153
Iser, 8, 139, 151, 162

J

Jakobson, 114, 142, 153, 159
Jeffries, 8, 121, 139
Johnson, vii, 5, 8, 139, 140

K

Karlsson, xiv, 139
Kiwan, 8, 140
knowledge, 8, 95, 98, 103, 109, 111, 126, 127, 129, 151, 152, 153, 155, 158, 159
Kress, 8, 95, 140
Kristeva, 119, 156

L

Lakoff, vii, 8, 122, 140
Lawrenson, 7, 140
learning, xvi, 7, 8, 93, 94, 95, 96, 97, 98, 105, 108, 130, 136, 137, 140, 141, 142, 144, 146, 153, 158
lecturing, 8, 94, 95, 96, 97, 134, 137, 145, 156, 157
Leech, 4, 140
Levinson, 8, 135
Lindsay, 94, 140
linguistic, 4, 8, 103, 104, 105, 106, 108, 109, 110, 113, 114, 120, 122, 126, 127, 140, 147, 154, 158
literary, xiii, xiv, xv, 5, 6, 8, 105, 109, 113, 117, 119, 129, 135, 136, 141, 142, 143, 147, 150, 151, 156, 157, 158, 159, 160, 161, 162
literature, xiv, xvi, 6, 8, 111, 117, 134, 136, 138, 139, 141, 142, 145, 146, 151, 155, 156, 157, 158, 160, 161, 162
lockdown, xvi, 8, 143, 152, 157
Locke, xiv, 133, 139
Longhurst, 4, 133
Lorini, 8, 95, 141
love, xv, 6, 7, 8, 94, 106, 129, 133, 139, 142, 148, 149, 152, 160, 162
Lucas, 8, 145
Lumpkin, 8, 141
Luther, xvi, 8, 130, 133, 137, 158
lyric, xvii, 8

M

Mallon, 8, 141
manner, xiii, 3, 4, 8, 103, 108, 119
Martins, 8, 141
Maslow, 8, 141
Matoesian, 8, 141
Matthiessen, 8, 138

maxim, 8, 126
McFarland, 8, 141
McIntosh, 8, 141
McLuhan, 8, 141
meaning, xiv, xv, xvi, 4, 5, 8, 93, 95, 101, 102, 103, 104, 105, 106, 108, 109, 114, 117, 121, 124, 126, 130, 131, 133, 137, 138, 139, 149, 150, 162
media, xiv, 4, 8, 110, 113, 114, 116, 125, 127, 131, 133, 135, 141, 157
medieval age, 8, 93, 95, 98, 130
medium, 4, 8, 141
memory, xv, 8, 147, 150
Merton, 8, 141
message, 8, 94, 114, 122, 136, 141
metaphor, 5, 8, 117, 118, 124, 133, 139, 140
method, 8, 94, 95, 96, 97, 98, 130, 134, 146, 149, 153
Mey, 8, 141
Meyer, xiii, 8, 141, 143
Mishra, 8, 141
mode, 5, 8, 140, 153
monist, 3, 4
Moroni, 8, 95, 141
motivation, xv, xvii, 8, 141
mystic, 155, 160

N

narrative, xv, xvii, 8, 123, 129, 133, 138, 157
nature, xv, 6, 7, 8, 103, 108, 147, 159, 162
neologism, 120
non-literary, xiv, xvi, 101, 109, 117, 129, 131, 151
Nordkvelle, 95, 142
Nørgaard, 8, 142
noun, 103, 104, 123
Nunan, xvii

O

O'Meara, xv, 8, 157
objectivity, xv, 8, 151

P

Packer, 8, 142
painting, vii, ix, xiii, xv, xvi, 4, 7, 8, 93, 95, 97, 98, 130, 139, 157
pandemic, xvi, xvii, 8, 130, 134, 152, 157
parallelism, 8, 102, 103, 105, 117, 148
Parsons, 8, 142
participant, 8, 149
Paz, 8, 142
peace, 6, 8, 95, 105, 120, 122, 127, 137, 148
pedagogy, 8, 98, 134
perspective, xv, 4, 8, 104, 105, 138, 139, 145
Philpot, 8, 142
Plato, xiv, 8, 135
pluralist, 3, 4
poem, xiii, xv, xvi, 7, 8, 106, 107, 129, 130, 139, 140, 143, 148, 149, 150, 152, 157, 158, 160, 161
pragmatic, xv, 8, 103, 105, 129, 142, 150
process, xv, 8, 96, 116, 120, 126, 149, 153
pronoun, 8, 121, 139, 149
pyramid, vii, 8, 152

R

Rashdall, 8, 142
Ray, 8, 142
reader-response, xvi, 8, 130, 136, 151, 158, 162

reading, xiii, xv, xvi, 8, 95, 101, 103, 105, 107, 114, 121, 129, 130, 139, 145, 150, 151, 152, 157, 158
reception, 8, 109, 115, 135, 151, 162
reception theory, 3, 162
reflection, 8, 102, 104, 105, 108, 109, 143, 148, 149
register, vii, xvi, 8, 108, 153
Reisigl, 96, 143
repetition, 8, 102, 120
representation, xvi, 8, 93
rheme, 94
rhetoric, xv, 8, 116, 122, 127, 138, 139
rhythm, 8, 147
Ribière, 8, 143
Richards, 8, 157
Robinson, 7, 143
Rosenblatt, 8, 143, 158
rubric, 8
Rumi, 8, 143, 160
Rymes, 8, 143

S

Schapiro, 4, 143
Schmitt, 103, 143
Schulpbach, 8
Seidensticker, 8, 141
sentence, 8, 102, 104, 106, 108, 117, 123
Sepmeyer, 8, 143
Shakespeare, 8, 106, 107, 150
Shelley, 6, 150, 157, 159
Shi, 8, 144
Shklovsky, 8, 161
Short, 4, 140, 144
simile, 8, 117, 148
Simpson, 8, 144
situational, 8
skill, 8

Socrates, 8
Spielvogel, 8, 136
Stafford, 8, 135
structure, 8, 102, 103, 106, 108, 110, 117, 123
style, xiii, xiv, xv, xvi, xvii, 3, 4, 5, 6, 8, 94, 95, 97, 101, 102, 103, 105, 106, 108, 109, 110, 115, 116, 117, 127, 128, 129, 130, 131, 133, 138, 147, 148, 149, 150, 152, 154
stylistics, xiv, 8, 103, 110, 117, 133, 134, 135, 142, 145, 146
subjectivity, xv, xvii, 8, 128, 131
sublime, 5
Suen, 8
symbol, 6, 139, 150

T

Tagore, 8
Tait, 94, 137
teaching, xiii, xvi, 7, 8, 94, 95, 96, 97, 98, 110, 129, 130, 133, 137, 138, 140, 141, 143, 146, 158, 160
tenor, 8, 153
text, xv, xvii, 8, 103, 104, 109, 110, 113, 115, 116, 117, 129, 131, 138, 139, 143, 151, 157, 158, 162
theme, xvi, 8, 94, 106, 152, 153
thinking, xiii, xvii, 8, 97, 104, 109, 131, 138
tone, xv, 4, 8, 114, 115
transaction, 8, 158
trope, 8, 103, 122, 126

U

understanding, 8, 95, 105, 109, 116, 117, 129, 133
utterance, 114

V

Valli, 8, 145
Van Dijk, 8, 96, 145
verb, 8, 102, 103, 149
vertical, 8, 129
Voltolina, 8, 97, 130, 157

W

Wales, 4, 145
Wan, 96, 145
Warren, 8, 141
Weingarten, 8, 145
Wodak, 96, 143
Wordsworth, 7, 147, 159, 160, 161
writers, xvi, 5, 8, 110, 113, 117, 126, 127, 128, 154

Y

Yeats, xv, 8, 159, 161

Z

Zeng, 8, 146

www.ingramcontent.com/pod-product-compliance
Lightning Source LLC
Chambersburg PA
CBHW051525230426
43668CB00012B/1745